Conversations With Jesus

365 Daily Devotions for Teens

by Lisa Cheater

Have you ever wondered what Jesus would say to teens if He could email or text them every day?

God never intended for us to journey through life alone or without direction, and Conversations with Jesus is the perfect tool for every teen who desires to know more about Jesus and what the Bible says about any life situation. Through a collection of encouraging, quick-read messages written in Jesus' first-person voice, Conversations with Jesus helps teens turn "religion" into a real "relationship" with Christ. Each day, students ages 12-18 are guided toward a closer walk with their Savior through a full year of carefully selected scripture passages and relevant applications that are trustworthy, practical, and action-oriented. Through Conversations with Jesus, teens will:

♥ *Develop a closer, more personal relationship with Jesus*

♥ *Be encouraged through tough times*

♥ *Discover how to handle difficult people*

♥ *Develop a clearer sense of God's will for their lives*

♥ *Learn how surrender leads to joy regardless of one's circumstances*

♥ *Understand how the Bible applies to daily life*

♥ *Become equipped to encourage others*

♥ *Become more comfortable with prayer as a response to Jesus.*

Jesus is waiting to talk with you today, and He's already prepared a message just for you. Are you willing to open it?

Published by Christian Devotions Ministries
P.O. Box 6494
Kingsport, TN, 37663

www.christiandevotions.us
http://lighthousepublishingofthecarolinas.com
books@christiandevotions.us

Published in association with Lighthouse Publishing of the Carolinas

ISBN: 978-0-9847655-1-5

Conversations With Jesus: 365 Daily Devotions for Teens

All scripture quotations, unless otherwise indicated, are taken from the New American Standard Bible®, Copyright © 1960, 1962, 1963, 1968, 1971, 1972, 1973, 1975, 1977, 1995 by The Lockman Foundation. Used by permission. All NIV references are from the HOLY BIBLE, NEW INTERNATIONAL VERSION®. NIV®. Copyright © 1973, 1978, 1984 by International Bible Society. Used by permission of Zondervan. All rights reserved.

Published by: Christian Devotions Ministries:
www.christiandevotions.us

Praise for Conversations With Jesus

"Our students find the subject matter covered in *Conversations with Jesus: 365 Daily Devotions for Teens* relative to where they are...They <u>want</u> action steps in a devotional, things to think and pray about." - **Bobby Gatlin**, Minister to Students - Johnson Ferry Baptist Church

"Teens are looking for someone to listen to them, not judge, and the devotions in *Conversations with Jesus* are really set up to encourage a relationship with Christ as a loving Lord. And because they can receive the content digitally, students are more likely to fit quiet time into their daily life." - **Debra Poston**, *Student Group Leader - Johnson Ferry Baptist Church*

Lisa Cheater *Biosketch*

An award-winning professional writer, Lisa is founder and CEO of The Penstock Group, Inc., a communications firm that specializes in film and print. With more than 20 years experience in business to business writing and visual media, Lisa's published work includes trade reports, industry articles, and short stories. She is a frequent writer-for-hire for the North American Mission Board (NAMB) and received two Emmy® Awards as writer for *"On Mission Xtra" (2009-11)*, a faith-based television series, and a television documentary entitled *"A New Hope" (2010)*.

Lisa is an active ministry leader for women's events, music, drama, video production, and missions at her home church, Johnson Ferry Baptist Church (JFBC), in Atlanta. A dedicated prayer warrior, Lisa has also served as a Moms in Touch International area prayer coordinator and group leader since 2003, and has taught teens and moms how to improve the effectiveness of their prayer lives using Biblical principles.

A summa cum laude graduate from Mercer University with a BA in visual communications and minors in psychology and religion, Lisa studied marketing at Georgia State University. She is a member of the National Academy of Television Arts and Sciences, Women in Film Atlanta, Moms in Touch International, Georgia Production Partnership, the Marietta Business Association, and serves on the Advisory Board for Change-R-Hearts, Inc., a non-profit food rescue charity.

She and her husband Tom are the proud (and busy) parents of teenage boy/girl twins and a hyperactive dog who love to hike, swim, and create music. The family resides near Atlanta, Georgia.

by Lisa Cheater

Introduction

Every day, you have a message waiting from Jesus. Will you open it?

Have you ever wished you could actually hear God's voice? Wouldn't it be cool to call Him up on a cell phone like you do your best friend, or receive emails and text messages direct from Jesus whenever you have a problem?

Believe it or not, Jesus has an instant messaging service for every Christian. He communicates directly with you every day through the Bible, other Christians, godly parents, teachers, authorities, and church leaders, but as frantically busy young people, it can be tough to halt all the distractions in your life long enough to hear His words.

The solution? Train your heart to listen more carefully and practice talking to God.

Not Your Mama's Devotional

A *devotional* is a message, either written or spoken, that helps you live out your devotion to Christ. Scripture is used in a devotion, but the Bible is so much more than just a collection of ordinary words. It strengthens and corrects, guides and uplifts. Scripture is the voice of the Lord in written form. Though the world's messages are often confusing,

I

contradictory, and deadly, you can trust what you read in scripture as direction for your life. Here's why:

1) It's true - *("For the Word of the LORD is right and true;"* - **Psalm 33:4 NIV)**

2) It never fails - *("...My word that goes out from my mouth...will not return to me empty, but will accomplish what I desire and achieve the purpose for which I sent it."* - **Isaiah 55:11 NIV)**

3) It is God's voice - *("All Scripture is God-breathed and is useful for teaching, rebuking, correcting and training in righteousness."* - **2 Timothy 3:16 NIV)**

You can learn to hear the Lord's voice no matter where you are, and just like playing an instrument or sport, chatting with Jesus takes just a little practice and discipline. This book is an excellent tool to help you get started. Flipping to today's message is like speed-dialing God: it's an instant connection! *"Conversations with Jesus"* contains thoughts the Lord wants to share with teens like you, organized in a format that fits your busy schedule. Follow along each day, and you'll be amazed how the words coincide with what you are going through at that moment. Look for it. Expect it. These short messages and Life Situquations™ (formulas that make quick sense out of complex Christian concepts) will help you navigate the unique challenges facing teens, grow in your faith as a Christian, and wise up to God's will for your life.

As in any relationship, communication is a two-way street. Once you've read the day's scripture and Jesus' message for you, it's your turn to talk. You can use the suggested prayer or come up with your own, just as long as you reply back to Jesus about how that day's devotion speaks to your heart and how you will apply it to your life.

Double-check Your Team Status

The first step is to ask yourself this question: "Who is *really* Lord of my life?" This devotional book is geared for Christians, those who have consciously decided to follow Jesus Christ as their Lord and Savior.

by Lisa Cheater

Simply believing that Jesus was a nice Jewish guy and brilliant teacher is not the same as trusting Him with your life. If you have not made Jesus ruler of your life, there are just a few simple steps to becoming a Believer, a Christian:

1) Admit you aren't perfect. Sin separates you from God and His blessings. That's the bad news. *("For all have sinned and fall short of the glory of God." - **Romans 3:23**)*

2) The *good* news (aka, The Gospel) is that our Holy God provided a way for you to be forgiven of your sins and communicate with Him through the death and resurrection of His son, Jesus. *("...But the gift of God is eternal life through Jesus Christ our Lord." - **Romans 6:23b**)*

3) Do you believe that Jesus died for you and has the power to forgive? Then ask Him to come into your heart to guide your life! *("Whoever will call on the name of the Lord will be saved!" - **Romans 10:13**)*

4) Go tell someone about the new relationship you just began with Christ!

If you accepted Christ as a very young child, it could be time to refresh your commitment to Him. Maybe things aren't going the way you'd hoped, or your behavior and attitude fall way short of where you'd like them to be. Look back through the steps above and pray through each one as a renewal of your faith. God can rekindle the spark you first felt as a new Believer and give you the desire to make each day forward count for Him!

Now get set to bring the power of Christ into your life through scripture and daily devotion!

There's a message waiting for you today...all you have to do is read!

Forget the past . . .

"I am focusing all my energies on this one thing: Forgetting the past and looking forward to what lies ahead." - **Philippians 3:13b**

Every day offers you a brand new start. Are there things you'd like to correct? Maybe you regret saying harsh words to someone yesterday or doing a few things last week you now find embarrassing. Confess to Me the behaviors you want to transform. Uttering those first words of repentance is really tough, but that's the place to start. The past has no hold over you once you place it into My hands. Once I forgive you, I totally forget your mistakes, and that's what I want you to do.

> Now What? *Pray:* "Lord, help me find courage now to admit to you the things I have done wrong. Forgive me for failing to abide by your loving commandments, for rebelling against you, and for doubting your sovereign power. Allow me to forgive myself, forgive others, and grow closer to you each day."

by Lisa Cheater

The ultimate mobile gift...

"Each one should use whatever gift he has received to serve others, faithfully administering God's grace in its various forms." - **1 Peter 4:10 (NIV)**

Do you remember what you received for Christmas last year? Two years ago? I give every Believer very special gifts that will never be destroyed, stolen at school, or forgotten in the back of a closet. First, you receive the assurance of eternal life with Me in Heaven, and second, every Christian gets at least one unique spiritual skill or talent. Maybe it's singing, teaching, prayer, faithfulness, joy, caretaking, leadership, hospitality - there are so many! Think about the skills I have blessed you with, and commit to use them every day this year.

Now What? *Pray:* "Jesus, thank you for the abilities you have given me! I know I am unique and special because you love me so much. Prevent me from comparing myself to others, and, instead, help me find ways to use my gifts in ways that please you and lead the lost toward a relationship with you."

I can hear you now . . .

"Then Jonah prayed to the LORD his God from the stomach of the fish..." - **Jonah 2:1**

Unlike cell phone coverage, your prayers reach Me no matter where you are. My prophet Jonah was swallowed by a whale around the year 785 B.C., and he cried out to Me from inside its stomach. I heard his cry for help, and I commanded the fish to spit him out on a beach. True story! You can pray to Me any time, day or night, and from any place— at home or at school, on a date or with friends—and I will hear you.

> Now What? *Pray:* "Jesus, I admit that I often forget to ask you for help because I can't see or touch you. But I do trust your power, and I know you are the same God who performed the amazing miracles recorded in the Bible. Lord, I come to you right now with this big problem: ___(name it)_____. I ask you to grant me wisdom and peace as I turn this situation over to you. Show me the right way to handle it and to remember that you are in control over all things."

by Lisa Cheater

Blessing insurance . . .

"Children, obey your parents in the Lord, for this is right. 'Honor your father and mother'--which is the first commandment with a promise, that it may go well with you and that you may enjoy long life on the earth." - **Ephesians 6:1-3 (NIV***)*

Life Situquation #1: Respect for your Parents +
Self Control = Blessing of God's Favor

Now What? *Pray:* "Help me, Lord, to be courteous and respectful to my parents and others today. I ask for your control over my words and attitude, especially when I am angry or disappointed. Let me be a solid ambassador for you so that others will see something different, something positive, in me."

True BFF . . .

" ...a real friend sticks closer than a brother." - **Proverbs 18:24**

It's a great blessing to have a pal who knows you better than anyone else, someone who keeps your secrets and encourages you. Sometimes, though, even your best buddies can let you down. Because I already know all your secrets, nothing shocks or surprises Me about you. I'll never leave you nor drop you like a hot rock! The Bible is full of all kinds of true stories about what I was like when I lived on earth. Those stories are meant to help you get to know Me. So, the next time you feel the need to run to your best friend with a problem, run to Me first.

Now What? *Pray:* "Jesus, you are the only one who can actually solve my problems. And your way is always right! I ask for your guidance with this issue: _____ (name it)_____. Stop me from worrying about this problem, reveal to me through scripture what I should do, and surround me with other Believers who can encourage me and provide direction."

by Lisa Cheater

Can do!

"For nothing will be impossible with God." - **Luke 1:37**

Why do you worry and complain when faced with a challenge? My Father, who created the entire universe, can see you through every adversity, and My word is full of direction in any circumstance. Don't try to manage life all by yourself! Challenges are always opportunities for you to grow in faith and confidence. Tackle that problem with assurance knowing that I am in control and more than strong enough to guide you.

Now What? *Pray:* "Lord, I confess that I do not enjoy life challenges! Give me faith in your power and help me approach my problems with joy. Take away my fears of failure and humiliation and replace those feelings with peace and confidence."

Life's like a rollercoaster . . .

"Do not let your heart be troubled; believe in God, believe also in Me."-
John 14:1

Life often feels like a wild ride on a mega-thrill roller coaster,
full of super highs and terrifying lows. Without control over the coaster,
your only option is to hang on and ride! You will have many experiences
like that as you mature. Sometimes life is wonderful and exhilarating,
and other times it seems like things are spinning off track. I'm like your
lap bar on that runaway coaster! Cling tightly to Me, especially during
crazy times, and I will hold you together.

Now What? *Pray:* "Jesus, life is so hard on this earth, but
I thank you for being steady when everything else seems
so chaotic. I will cling to you because I know your ways
are always best for me, even when I don't understand
how you're working in my life. Knowing that, Lord,
I choose to calm my mind and kick my worries to the
curb. Right now."

by Lisa Cheater

Unpack . . .

"Therefore confess your sins to each other and pray for each other so that you may be healed. The prayer of a righteous man is powerful and effective."- **James 5:16 (NIV)**

You know how you hate to unpack your duffle bag after trips, and all your stuff stays in there for weeks until your Mom finally makes you take it all out so it can be washed? Maybe you're dreading what you might find in there (like a half-eaten candy bar). Today I'd like you to unpack your heart. You have stuff in there like unconfessed sin, anger, bitterness, worry, rebellion, and confusion, and like that candy bar, that junk can really start to reek over time; it can make you depressed and irritable. Unpack all that resentfulness, and let Me forgive you. If you want, go talk to a youth minister or Bible teacher. Once you unpack, you and I will be closer, and you'll feel like a huge weight has been lifted off your shoulders, just like that icky duffle.

Now What? *Pray:* "Lord, you see everything and you know all about me. You know what sins I hide, but I can't keep living a lie. I want to be free of the enemy's power over me in this area of my life: ____(name it)____. I confess this to you and accept your promise of forgiveness! Keep me from temptation, protect me, and give me the courage to change this behavior. Thank you, Lord Jesus, for loving me so much."

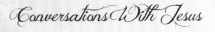

The shoe fits . . .

"Ask, and it will be given to you; seek, and you will find; knock, and it will be opened to you. For everyone who asks receives, and he who seeks finds, and to him who knocks it will be opened." - **Matthew 7:7-8**

Remember the story of Cinderella? The Prince searched everywhere for the maiden whose dainty foot fit the lost glass slipper. Adolescents can be just like that Prince. The early teen years are a time for you to begin learning about your true personality, and you may try on different activities, friends, styles and slang until one seems to "fit." Look to Me as your ultimate source of affirmation, and don't try to be someone you're not! I adore you exactly as you have been created.

Now What? *Pray:* "Jesus, I know in my mind you created me special and perfect in your sight, but I can't help being envious of: ____(name person)_____. I feel so inferior compared to him/her. But I also know those feelings are lies from the evil one, sent to discourage my faith in you. Lord, please erase my self-doubt and remind me of the promises in your Word! I give you, this very moment, my identity, my plans, my personality, my appearance, my skills, and my words. Help me use them for good. Thank you for how you've made me."

by Lisa Cheater

Live out loud ...

"Whoever has My commands and obeys them, he is the one who loves Me. He who loves me will be loved by My Father, and I too will love him and show myself to him." - **John 14:21 (NIV)**

Your love for Me is shown in many ways: prayer, worship, attitude, and obedience. It's not an easy ride. Keeping My commandments and My words in your heart as a guide for how to behave can be really hard, but when you live out your belief in Me through your words and actions, the world can easily see that your faith is real. Don't keep hope to yourself. Show kindness to someone today.

Now What? *Pray:* "Jesus, thank you for being the perfect example of love in action. Give me the opportunity today to express my gratitude by being kind to someone else. May that person be blessed by my words and deeds."

Always do your best...

"... know that from the Lord you will receive the reward of the inheritance. It is the Lord Christ whom you serve." - **Colossians 3:24**

You cannot pick and choose who you want to work hard for and who you skimp on. As My follower, I want you to see every task you're given - from housework to schoolwork, from sports to music - as an assignment from Me. I want you to give everything your best, not so people will be impressed, but because you love Me. Give every outcome to Me as an offering of your love, and you will be blessed with the satisfaction of a job well done.

Now What? *Pray:* "I know you have given me specific talents, Lord. Forgive me for not using them wisely and for not doing my best in tasks I find boring or uninteresting. Help me put aside the need for others' approval and my quest for constant 'happiness'. Jesus, grant me the diligence to always do my very best."

by Lisa Cheater

Perfection not a prerequisite . . .

"But God demonstrates His own love toward us, in that while we were yet sinners, Christ died for us." - **Romans 5:8**

I didn't die for saints, I died for sinners! Long before you chose Me, I chose you. I knew one day you would read these very words and would need My protection and love to make it through a difficult world. Best of all, My love is not dependent upon how good you are. I can give you the desire and ability to love others, but My love for you never ends, even when you make mistakes. That's the awesome nature of grace.

Now What? *Pray:* "God, it's hard for me to comprehend a love so pure that it doesn't require perfection! I often feel too inadequate to be in your presence, yet I know my salvation and faith can never be taken from me. I am so grateful for your acceptance of me that is not contingent upon how good I am or how many generous deeds I rack up. Forgive me for failing to accept that you love me totally, faults and all."

13

Shine on!

"Then Jesus again spoke to them, saying, 'I am the Light of the world; he who follows Me will not walk in the darkness, but will have the Light of life.'" - **John 8:12**

Just as your eyes would strain to locate any spark of light in the total darkness of a cave, I am the Light in a dark, sinful world. People may seem happy on the outside, but inside, most are searching for some glimmer of hope and truth. You are like a lit match sent to illuminate the way for others. Don't hide your light by being a chameleon, changing your behavior to suit whoever is around. Let your faith shine through your behavior every day.

Now What? *Pray:* "Lord, you are a perfect light, full of hope and joy. I am grateful for those in my life who are encouraging examples of your goodness, like: ____(name a godly person you respect)____. Thank you for reminding me that someone else may be watching me closely, too, and to make sure my behavior mirrors my heart."

by Lisa Cheater

14

Academics are a part...

"Acquire wisdom! Acquire understanding! Do not forget nor turn away from the words of my mouth." - **Proverbs 4:5**

It's important to do your best in school so you'll understand how the world works, but head-knowledge alone won't make you wise. True wisdom comes from hearing, reading, remembering, and living out My teachings. It's not enough to simply believe I am the Son of God; even demons acknowledge that fact! The challenge is to make Me Lord of your actions and choices. Stay plugged into My Word and you will know how to answer any life-question that comes your way.

Now What? *Pray:* "Lord Jesus, I have so much to do, and so many assignments begging for my attention! School is sometimes really tough for me, especially: ____(name a subject or activity)____. Grant me wisdom, Lord, and help me make time in my schedule for rest and quiet time with your word."

Easy access...

"You drew near when I called on You; You said, 'Do not fear!'" - **Lamentations 3:57**

You'll never get a busy signal from Me. I don't have call waiting or a holy hold button, and you won't have to call back because I'm out of town. Any hour of every day, I am only a breath away. I love talking with you and hearing about all the things that are on your heart right now, the good and the bad (you can't hide your thoughts from Me, so be honest). I am always accessible as your comforter and friend.

Now What? *Pray:* "Jesus, I love knowing you can always hear my prayer, *this* prayer, right now! I often forget how easy it is to talk with you and that you want to hear from me. I want to tell you two things right now. First, I am so thankful for ____(name it)____, and second, I need your help with ____(name it)____. Thank you, Lord, for scripture and leaders that provide answers for every situation."

by Lisa Cheater

No taking back . . .

"But when he asks, he must believe and not doubt, because he who doubts is like a wave of the sea, blown and tossed by the wind." - **James 1:6 (NIV)**

You say you believe I can do anything, so why do you doubt? Right after you ask Me to help you, you immediately think, "Yeah, right. God can't fix this." Instead of feeling confident and at peace after praying, you feel just as unsettled as you did before! Why? When you ask something of Me, give it to Me completely, without a doubt, and you can be certain I will handle it.

> Now What? *Pray:* "I admit that I struggle with doubt, Jesus. I'm learning to record and study observations in science, and yet I cannot see you! Faith is so weird! Teach me to let go of my problems once I place them in your care, and to avoid second-guessing your power just because I can't understand how you work."

17

It's okay to be angry . . .

"Be angry and yet do not sin; do not let the sun go down on your anger, and do not give the devil an opportunity." - **Ephesians 4:26-27**

Everyone feels angry at times. I made you to respond to injustice with anger and to feel all kinds of emotions. When anger prompts you to help people or to speak out against evil, it's a good thing. The line is crossed when angry emotions become angry actions. Hateful words, tantrums, breaking My commandments, and gossip are not okay. Anger can grow and spread in your heart like a disease, which is exactly what the enemy wants for you. Instead, talk to Me when you've had enough of the world, and I will lift your burdens.

Now What? *Pray:* "Lord God, I understand that angry outbursts are not pleasing to you, but sometimes I can't seem to help myself. Nothing pushes my buttons more than: ____(name it)____! Show me where I am at fault, and forgive me for overreacting. Give me courage to make amends with others wherever possible and to let your Holy Spirit override my desire to explode in anger."

by Lisa Cheater

Keep Me first...

"You shall have no other gods before Me." - **Exodus 20:3**

When Moses lived thousands of years ago, people worshipped gods and idols other than Me, and the result was always disastrous. Just like today. You may not worship some golden calf statue, but what about your obsessions, preoccupations with celebrities, bands, dating, clothes, or just "stuff?" Anything that takes My place and becomes more important to you than anything else, is an idol. Keep Me number one so I can bless you beyond your expectations.

Now What? *Pray:* "Thank you, Lord, for the intelligence you've given people to create some really cool stuff. I realize, though, material possessions can never fill the needs of my heart the way you can. I give my preoccupation with earthly objects to you right now, and I ask you to replace my obsession with a desire to know you more."

Set a goal . . .

"And let us run with endurance the race that God has set before us." - **Hebrews 12:1b**

What's one "thing" you'd really like to transform about yourself or your behavior (something you can actually change, NOT your height or your shoe size!). Would you like to be more patient? Or maybe stop gossiping about others? Got it in mind? Make that your goal for this year. It'll be hard because it's a habit that's become part of your character. Think of it as a race, where your goal is the finish line. You'll have to stay focused—day by day, step by step, mile by mile—but with Me, you can do it. Don't give up.

> Now What? *Pray:* "You alone, God, are able to change me from the inside out. I want to have a character that pleases you, so I ask you to help me change my _____ (name specific behavior)_____. I know it won't be easy and it won't happen overnight, so please help me stay encouraged and to take one day at a time."

by Lisa Cheater

Seek Me first . . .

"But seek first His kingdom and His righteousness, and all these things will be added to you." - **Matthew 6:33**

Think about the word, "seek." It means to look for something really hard, just like those games of hide and seek you used to play when you were little. Unlike your sly playmates, though, it's easy to seek and find Me. How? Just stop and pray. When you consult Me first and set My kingdom as your number one priority, I promise to provide everything you will ever need. And then some!

Now What? *Pray:* "God, sometimes I don't know what I need, I just know I feel lousy and unhappy for no apparent reason. Being a teen can be so confusing. Bring me back to the things that allow me to grow closer to you: reading your Word, listening at church, and really participating in worship rather than just bobbing to the beat of the music. Thank you for seeking *me* and for filling me with the peace of your presence."

Weapons allowed . . .

"...let us be sober, having put on the breastplate of faith and love, and as a helmet, the hope of salvation." - **1 Thessalonians 5:8**

The enemy is everywhere, looking for opportunities to entice you to sin and destroy relationships that build you up as a Believer, but hear this: I have not left you without mighty weapons to conquer any foe! Your faith in My strength is impenetrable, even in the worst of times, and the promise of salvation protects your mind from depression and self destruction. Don't let evil have easy access to your life. Keep your guard up and have faith in Me!

> Now What? *Pray:* "Jesus, I confess to you that I am frequently afraid of lots of things: failure, others' opinions of me, how I look, how smart I am... The need to fit in often makes me do things I shouldn't. I ask for your shield to surround and protect me against all the schemes and mind-games of the enemy. Because of the blood you shed on the cross, I am able to claim your power over my life and my thoughts, right this moment. Thank you, Lord, for your love."

by Lisa Cheater

One step at a time . . .

"For God is not a God of confusion but of peace..." - **1 Corinthians 14:33**

     I see every tear you cry and every heartbreak you feel. I know when pressure at school and at home seems too much to bear, when all your responsibilities mount up like a giant tidal wave, and it feels like there's nowhere to run. Fear and confusion are *not* from Me. Don't get so freaked out by all the deadlines that you can't figure out what to do next. Tell Me about your day and what frustrates you. Then, together, we can plan out your tasks for today.

     Now What? *Pray:* "Lord, help me see that how I spend my day is a reflection of what's in my heart. Show me where I need to focus my time today, and exclude from my schedule anything that is not a priority. Give me the courage to say 'no' to requests for my time that fall outside your will or cause overscheduling so that every moment of this day will count in service for you."

I'm all you need ...

"Make sure that your character is free from the love of money, being content with what you have; for He Himself has said, 'I will never desert you, nor will I ever forsake you.'" - **Hebrews 13:5**

Images and ads bombard you every day about the latest and greatest music device, phones, and computers. Advertisers are smart. They try to convince you that buying these things will bring you happiness and cool friends. But friendship with Me is the most valuable gift you can ever have because it can never be taken away. Never. Avoid letting jealousy into your heart. It only leads to unhappiness. Instead, be thankful for all I've given you, including My life.

Now What? *Pray:* "Father, you have given so much to me. I lose sight of all my blessings and forget that many people on this earth would consider me wealthy. I release the jealousy I feel for the things my friends have, and I thank you for the physical and spiritual gifts you've placed in my life. Help me use all I have to bring honor to your name."

by Lisa Cheater

Only the inside counts . . .

"Do not look at his appearance or at the height of his stature, because I have rejected him; for God sees not as man sees, for man looks at the outward appearance, but the LORD looks at the heart." - **1 Samuel 16:7**

Technology brings many good things into your life, but it also delivers many harmful messages that can cause you to feel discontented, doubtful, or unattractive. TV ads promise beauty and popularity, and unhealthily skinny actors and actresses make you feel like a gnarly tree stump in a glade of flowing willows. These are lies straight from Satan, tricks to make you doubt your worth and move your focus away from growing My kingdom! Serve Me, and only Me, and you will not need the world's stamp of approval.

Now What? *Pray:* "Jesus, thank you for seeing the beauty of a righteous heart, and for creating me uniquely perfect in your eyes. I will not insult your creativity by wishing I looked like someone else, for I know many people who are nice looking on the outside, but their hatefulness and arrogance make them unattractive. True beauty comes from godly character, so teach me to behave in a way that pleases you."

Table for two . . .

"But because of his great love for us, God, who is rich in mercy, made us alive with Christ even when we were dead in transgressions--it is by grace you have been saved." - **Ephesians 2:4-5 (NIV)**

The moment you believed in Me as your Savior, God lifted you out of the deadness of sin, just like He raised Me from the dead after three days, because He loves you so very much. This sounds like a science fiction tale, but it's real, trust Me. I died *for you* so you can experience forgiveness, real joy on earth, and glorious eternal life in Heaven!

Now What? *Pray:* "Lord, I praise your name as the one and only sure salvation. I don't need to worry or wonder if I'll make it into Heaven; you already fought that battle for me through your death and resurrection! Thank you for the promise of a life with you. Strengthen my faith so I can lead others to know you."

by Lisa Cheater

Dream big . . .

"Don't let anyone think less of you because you are young. Be an example to all believers in what you teach, in the way you live, in your love, your faith, and your purity." - **1 Timothy 4:12**

Why are you so determined to grow up quickly and experience life as an adult? You will *not* be a kid forever, so don't rush the process! I can work through people of all ages (remember, David was only twelve when he defeated the giant Goliath)! As a teen, you can be a powerful, effective witness for Me because you're surrounded by so many people who need salvation. Ask for My help, believing, and just see what we can accomplish together!

Now What? *Pray:* "Lord Jesus, I see now that this phase of my life is an important part of growing up and growing in faith. Don't let me waste the opportunities I have to share the Gospel! I know this friend needs to hear about you: ____(name friend)____. I pray this person's heart will become soft and open to hearing about your love. Give me the chance and strength to be a witness to him/her."

Do not worry . . .

"Do not be anxious about anything, but in everything, by prayer and petition, with thanksgiving, present your requests to God." - **Philippians 4:6 (NIV)**

All the things you hide in your heart, things you're afraid of, stuff you'd never tell your parents or your closest friend, are laid bare before My eyes. I already know all the sordid details, but I want you to tell Me about them anyway because it shows you trust Me. Fear and faith cannot exist together! There is power in My name and in My Word, the Bible. So, bring Me the stuff that worries you. I'll take care of it all.

Now What? *Pray:* "God, you are the only perfect remedy for all my anxieties. I worry so much over things I can't control, like: _____(name worry)_____, for example. It's really hard to say this, but I do thank you for what you're teaching me right now through this struggle. I don't get how you can do good things through my problems, but I given them to you and ask you to handle them for me. I can't do it. Strengthen my faith, Lord, and guide my next steps."

by Lisa Cheater

Be grateful for My discipline . . .

"God said, 'My child, don't ignore it when the Lord disciplines you, and don't be discouraged when he corrects you. For the Lord disciplines those he loves, and he punishes those he accepts as his children.'" - **Hebrews 12:4b-6**

What? Why would anyone be grateful for discipline? Here's why: I love you too much to let you wreck your life. You always have a choice to respond to My love and obey My Word, or to rebel. I discipline you through circumstances and individuals like your parents or authorities, and if you pay attention when you are in trouble, you may find that you broke My commands in some way. If I didn't love you, I'd let you have whatever you want and never protect you from harm. But I DO love you and will do what is best for you. Even if that means sometimes telling you, "no."

Now What? *Pray:* "Jesus, I understand now that sometimes the chaos in my life is caused by my own inattention to your direction. There are times when it seems doors are closing left and right, and everything I pursue ends up in disappointment. Rather than feeling discouraged, help me learn to see those closed doors as protection from you. Please keep leading me!"

Sorry vs. wrong . . .

"For the sorrow that is according to the will of God produces a repentance without regret..." - **2 Corinthians 7:10**

How many times have you told someone told you were sorry for something, but you didn't really mean it? Most people regret getting *caught*, not what they did wrong. Just uttering the word, "Sorry," is not genuine repentance. If you want forgiveness, admit you were wrong, change your attitude, and learn from the experience. Think about what you should have done instead, and ask for My help to avoid repeating the same mistake.

> Now What? *Pray:* "Lord, I don't want to rebel against your teachings because it only leads to conflict and sorrow. Convict my heart now with the name of a person I have wronged. Give me the courage to admit my shortcomings to you first, then to ask forgiveness from that individual. Thank you, Lord, for loving me and for offering second chances."

by Lisa Cheater

30

Appreciate your body...

"Don't you know that your body is the temple of the Holy Spirit, who lives in you and was given to you by God?" - **1 Corinthians 6:19**

Do you know what I call your body? A temple. It's like a church, a place that houses My spirit. You are often critical about what you see in the mirror, but I didn't make a mistake when I made you. I created you exactly the way you are and I am so proud of you. To Me, you are beautiful and perfect! That's why I want you to take care of yourself, My house. Eat healthy, be active, stay sexually pure, and avoid destructive behaviors like doing drugs and alcohol. Remember, whatever you do to your body, you do to Me.

Now What? *Pray:* "Father, help me remember the importance of taking care of myself, to rest, to fuel my body with healthy foods, and make wise choices. Today, replace my self-critical attitude with appreciation, and my dissatisfaction with gratitude. To start, one thing I really like about myself is: ____(name it)____. Lord, thank you for making me so wonderfully amazing."

Helpful talk . . .

"Do not let any unwholesome talk come out of your mouths, but only what is helpful for building others up according to their needs, that it may benefit those who listen." - **Ephesians 4:29 (NIV)**

Do you spend more time hurling insults and fighting with others than you do complimenting and praising them? What about at home? Your commitment to Me shows through the way you treat others. Calling people names is hurtful and it destroys your Christian witness. Today, try to say only things that are helpful, honest, and kind. It's a win-win: you'll be blessed by blessing others.

Now What? *Pray:* "Jesus, at times, I can't seem to stop myself from saying destructive things, but I realize I don't *have* to react with spite when I feel threatened. I have a choice. Lord, I do not have the power to control my tongue by myself. I desperately need your Holy Spirit to rule over my thoughts and my speech. Today, let my mouth speak only words of hope and help."

by Lisa Cheater

Get it together ...

"Then God said, 'Let there be an expanse in the midst of the waters, and let it separate the waters from the waters.'" - **Genesis 1:6**

I laid out the whole universe in careful order just to make the earth inhabitable, with every element, every plant and moon in its proper place. You are so busy each day, and I watch you absently lay things down as you rush about. It takes time to keep your stuff organized, but the reward is peace. You won't have to scramble around to find things at the last minute, and keeping your room orderly will make your parents happy because it shows you respect them. Staying organized is one small way you show your love for Me.

Now What? *Pray:* "Father, God, I've never really stopped to think about how you have organized the universe. You are creative and clever, and I am amazed by your power and attention to the smallest detail of everything in my life. Prompt me to spend some today time organizing my space and my time so I can glorify you through my obedience."

33

Day 33

Do your best . . .

"Work hard and cheerfully at whatever you do, as though you were working for the Lord rather than for people." - **Colossians 3:23**

Many things are on your agenda for this week. It's easy to put off things like school work and chores and concentrate on the easy, fun stuff. Sometimes you don't give your best effort because you don't think it matters, or you don't like the task. Transform your view of work! Complete your tough assignments as though I have personally assigned them to you, not a teacher or parent. I want you to do your best for Me, for My approval, not just theirs. You will feel awesome about yourself, and your excellence will be rewarded with success.

Now What? *Pray:* "Lord, search my heart and see that my true goal is to please you in everything I do and say. Forgive me for complaining about my school and home assignments, for you have placed these leaders in my path to teach and guide me. Help me see every task, even those I consider boring or mundane, as an opportunity to show my love for you."

by Lisa Cheater

Be ok with waiting ...

"Wait patiently for the LORD. Be brave and courageous. Yes, wait patiently for the LORD." - **Psalms 27:14**

I know you hate to wait. Standing in lines at your favorite amusement park ride, at a restaurant, or waiting for your birthday frustrates you. It's human nature to want things quickly and painlessly, but I want you to be strong in your faith, and sometimes, that requires time and waiting on Me. I am doing many wonderful things for you that you cannot yet see. I am preparing hearts, setting up situations, and molding you into the kind of person who can accept the blessings I have planned for you. So don't be discouraged! Just trust Me rather than wanting everything now.

Now What? *Pray:* "Yes, Lord, I do hate to wait for answers! Many times, I can't see your plan for my life and I don't understand why certain things happen, like _____(name a confusing situation)_____. Even though I don't completely understand how you work, I have faith that you're doing what's best for me and that things will work out better than I could ever imagine. Give me courage to push through times of waiting and to give you thanks when you choose to answer."

Last is better . . .

"Do nothing from selfishness or empty conceit, but with humility of mind regard one another as more important than yourselves;" - **Philippians 2:3**

Everyone wants the blue ribbon, the applause, the spotlight, but, as you're learning, the things that most please Me often involve going against human nature. I showed love to My disciples by washing their feet. You don't have to give pedicures to your buddies, but show love by offering your seat to an elderly woman, allowing your siblings to go in line before you, or giving time to help others. When you put others first, you come out on top.

> Now What? *Pray:* "Jesus, you became the ultimate example of selflessness when you died for me on the cross. How can I show my gratitude? Place someone in my path today that is in need of encouragement. Show me how best to help him or her, and may that person feel blessed because of my actions."

by Lisa Cheater

Praise the Father ...

"Sing to the LORD, all you godly ones! Praise his holy name." - **Psalms 30:4**

Think back to the concert or football game you last attended. Remember cheering so loud you nearly lost your voice? Few people praise Me with that kind of gusto. Praise is like dialing Me up on the phone. I am quick to respond when you praise My Father for all He has done and who He is. It's not complicated. Simply saying, "God, You are amazing. You are my Hope!" is praise!

> Now What? *Pray:* "You alone, God, are perfect and worthy of adoration. You, alone, are truly good and in control of every detail in my life. You, alone, proved more powerful than the grave, and I love you for loving me and all my imperfections. Thank you for valuing me as your chosen child."

Regroup . . .

"If we confess our sins, He is faithful and righteous to forgive us our sins and to cleanse us from all unrighteousness." - **1 John 1:9**

Everyone makes mistakes, but it's so easy for you to get wrapped up in pride and guilt. Every day I allow you to start fresh and new. Each morning you have the opportunity to confess your sins, and ask for forgiveness so I can give you a clean start for the day ahead. All I ask is that you work hard to avoid that particular sin in the future. Ask a Christian friend or leader to help you stand accountable for your behavior. We can do this, together.

Now What? *Pray:* "Jesus, I'm done blaming others for my sinful actions and behavior. No matter the situation, I always have the option to respond in a way that pleases you. Always. This is so hard for me, Lord, but because I want to be close to you, I confess to you these specific sins you've placed on my heart: ____ (name them) ____. Release me from these habits and reactions to stress, and help me make amends and ask forgiveness where necessary. Place in me a pure heart that desires to please only you."

by Lisa Cheater

38

Control your actions ...

"But the fruit of the Spirit is love, joy, peace, patience, kindness, goodness, faithfulness, gentleness, self-control..." - **Galatians 5:22-23**

Never assume that since you are My Follower, your life will be perfect. I cannot promise you a smooth ride, only that I will be with you for the journey. The world is full of evil and darkness. Your goal as My child is to demonstrate the fruits of My Spirit (above) in your life. Some of these characteristics may be hard for you, so talk to Me about which ones really stump you, and I will teach you to conquer them.

Now What? *Pray:* "Thank you, Jesus, for giving me clear goals for living through your Word! As I look at this list of nine spiritual fruits, proof that your Spirit is in me, I immediately know that I struggle with: _____ (name fruit(s) of the Spirit) _____. Today, help me substitute my natural selfish tendencies for your personality. Keep me from becoming frustrated with my growth as a Christian, and fill me with encouragement as I achieve small victories."

Keep My name Holy ...

"You shall not take the name of the LORD your God in vain, for the LORD will not leave him unpunished who takes His name in vain." - **Exodus 20:7**

It seems pretty harmless to blurt out, "OMG!" or "Jesus!" when something shocks you. But do you realize these outbursts are taking My name in vain, using it in a way that displeases Me? My name is special because I am the Holy God, the Messiah, your Savior! I rejoice over you when you breathe My name in prayer or in praise, so be an example to your friends by keeping this commandment and placing My powerful, precious name above all others.

Now What? *Pray:* "Lord, this is such a hard habit to break. Virtually everyone around me talks like this, or worse, everyday. Teach my tongue to obey you by speaking only clean, positive words that never show disrespect to you. Forgive me for all the times I've let curses slip or taken your name in vain. Allow me to become an example of light and goodness before my friends and family and to walk away from people that use bad language."

by Lisa Cheater

40

Don't be afraid ...

"In God, whose word I praise, In God I have put my trust; I shall not be afraid. What can mere man do to me?" - **Psalms 56:4**

Healthy fear alerts you to leave a dark alley or say "no" to an offer to do drugs, but an unhealthy fear can paralyze you into indecision. I have promised to watch over you whenever you call on Me. Know that I am beside you, even this very minute, and stop dwelling on a scenario that may not ever happen! The harsh words and actions of another person cannot harm you as long as you remember that I love and adore you.

Now What? *Pray:* "Lord, teach me to look to you whenever I feel afraid. Regardless of the situation, I know you can give me the courage to face my fear and follow through. Help me remember that this frightening time will pass, and tomorrow I can rejoice in knowing that I persevered with your help."

Be calm . . .

"And the peace of God, which surpasses all comprehension, will guard your hearts and your minds in Christ Jesus." - **Philippians 4:7**

Have you ever paid attention to how your body reacts to stress? Your palms sweat, your heart pounds, you can't think straight, and your throat tightens. Your body also reacts to calm thoughts. When you focus your mind on Me by praying or whispering words of thanks, your pulse slows, your breathing calms, and you feel relaxed. It's more than just meditation; it is My Holy Spirit filling you with peace.

Now What? *Pray:* "I long for that feeling of peace today, Jesus. I am easily overwhelmed and confused by the constant pressure of life, but you are my safe place, Lord, and I come to you now, like a ship that escapes a terrible storm and finds shelter in a safe harbor. Calm my frantic mind, still my restless heart, and focus my thoughts on the immediate task at hand."

by Lisa Cheater

Let it go . . .

"Submit therefore to God. Resist the devil and he will flee from you." -
James 4:7

"Everyone else is doing it" is not a valid excuse for any behavior. You are not a slave to sin! You have the ability to choose My way or Satan's. It's that simple. Each time you walk away from a potentially harmful situation or close your mouth instead of firing off insults, you have resisted the enemy and submitted to God! Faced with your courage, Satan has no choice but to turn-tail and run!

Now What? *Pray:* "God, I often feel like Satan is personally attacking me with discouragement and difficulty. Yet I know you are so much more powerful than anything! Through your name, I claim your power, and ask you to bind the enemy's attempts to make me doubt that you are real. Give me strength to resist temptation and wisdom to handle any challenges that come my way."

43

You are made perfectly ...

"I will give thanks to You, for I am fearfully and wonderfully made;" -
Psalms 139:14

"My nose is too big!" "I hate how short I am." "I wish I was skinny."
I hear complaints all the time from teens like you who are unhappy with
the way they look. But I made you perfectly. I formed you to be uniquely
YOU, not some other kid. To Me, you are all like a field of wildflowers that
are designed to be colored and shaped differently. Don't be fooled by the
retouched photographs in magazines that don't represent reality. Be grateful
for the differences that make you beautiful in My sight.

> Now What? *Pray:* "Lord, it's so hard not to compare
> my appearance to others around me. Sometimes I think I
> could improve upon your design of me, and I find myself
> wishing I were different. Better. Oh Lord, forgive me
> for criticizing your work! You created my physical
> makeup, personality, and abilities according to a perfect
> plan. Help me diligently seek your will as you reveal that
> plan to me."

by Lisa Cheater

Your real enemy . . .

"For our struggle is not against flesh and blood, but against the rulers, against the powers, against the world forces of this darkness, against the spiritual forces of wickedness in the Heavenly places." - **Ephesians 6:12**

You will constantly come in contact with people who are hurtful and maybe downright cruel. It's hard to feel love for them, but I want you to think of your enemies differently. The evil things they say and do are coming from a dark presence inside their heart because I am not there. Don't allow hate to take root in your thoughts. Pray for the enemy's grip on these people to be wrenched away, and for the lost to know Me as Lord. Love them as I love you.

Now What? *Pray:* "On my own, Lord, I do not have the capacity to love people who hurt me. Specifically, I have a huge problem with ____(name person)____ because this individual has wounded me so deeply in the past. First, allow me to let go of my pain and my resentment toward this person. Then, I ask you to reach inside this person's heart and free him/her from the influence of sin. Change my heart as I forgive this person."

Day of the heart ...

"Put to death, therefore, whatever belongs to your earthly nature: sexual immorality, impurity, lust, evil desires and greed, which is idolatry." - **Colossians 3:5 (NIV)**

Valentine's Day is all about romance, the joy of knowing someone loves you. There's nothing wrong with feeling affection for someone special, but don't buy into the popular idea that you must demonstrate your love to someone physically. Sex is reserved for a married man and woman. Anything else is against My will for your life. Not only can sex lead to pregnancy, but with the wrong individual, it can make you feel horrible about yourself. Commit to remain pure until you marry the person I have chosen for you. The wait will be worth it.

Now What? *Pray:* "Lord, images of love are all over the place today, visions of how the world interprets romance. I know your perfect love is the best, and that you have created an individual just for me. I'm way too young to worry about serious relationships right now, but I ask that you keep me physically pure until I meet that special someone and commit in marriage. Steer me away from destructive relationships and from dating anyone that falls outside your will for me."

by Lisa Cheater

Golden rule . . .

"You shall love your neighbor as yourself." - **Galatians 5:14**

All the Ten Commandments fit into two categories: Loving God and loving others. To love someone as much as you love yourself means you try to see things from their perspective, treating them the way you would want to be treated. Do you like to be made fun of, disrespected, and bullied? Neither do others. To show My love to people who don't know Me, be kind, joyful, courteous, and generous. They will want to know your secret: Me.

> Now What? *Pray:* "Lord, I know I am supposed to love others, and yet I often find myself sorting people into buckets of those I like and those I don't, those I'll be nice to and those I won't. I know this is not what your scripture teaches. One person I simply do not like is: ____(name them)____. Even if my reasons are justified, I pray for this person today and ask you to help me remember that you died for him/her just as you died for me."

47

Passing the buck ...

"Do not repay evil with evil or insult with insult, but with blessing..." -
1 Peter 3:9 (NIV)

Ever notice how anger can pass along from one person to the
next like a virus? The boss yells at the dad, the dad comes home
and yells at the kids, the kids kick the dog, then the dog probably
bites the neighbor. If someone has been cruel to you today, don't
pass it along! Give that situation to Me and resist the urge to carry
your anger home where you will likely hurt the people you love most.

Now What? *Pray:* "Jesus, I don't want to be seen as
weak and powerless in the eyes of those who hurt my
feelings or are unkind to me. It is so tempting to want to
seek revenge! But I will leave retaliation to you. Help
me resist the urge to pay back evil, and give me the faith
to leave my enemies in your capable hands. Guard my
tongue and my actions so that my behavior pleases you
despite what others around me do and say."

by Lisa Cheater

Avoid reacting in anger . . .

"My dear brothers and sisters, be quick to listen, slow to speak, and slow to get angry." - **James 1:19**

Hateful words occasionally fly out of your mouth like missiles from a Nerf gun, and once they're loose, the damage is done. I have placed relationships in your life to strengthen you, guide you, and build you up -- if you let them. There is great wisdom in the old adage: "count to ten" when you are angry. Let yourself calm down before you spit out a mean reaction that you'll probably regret.

Now What? *Pray:* "Lord, reverse everything I have learned from the world about the character of a strong person. I see now that in your eyes, the brute, the bully, the tyrant, is weak, and the one who hangs on to his composure and self-control is full of strength. That's how I want to become, and I will need your help. Fill me with your spirit and give me the boldness to walk away from arguments."

Watch out for pride . . .

"Blessed are the poor in spirit, for theirs is the kingdom of Heaven." -
Matthew 5:3

Being poor in spirit doesn't mean depressed. I value humbleness, a heart that is not prideful or full of itself. I can't hang out in the heart of someone who thinks they're better than others, who constantly gossips, or is mean-spirited. There simply isn't room for Me and their ego! Acknowledge Me as King so I can work in your life!

Now What? *Pray:* "Father, the phrase "humble teenager" seems like an impossible paradox. But you are God of the impossible! I ask you to empty me of my selfish desires, and fill me up with your Holy Spirit. I want your words to become my words, and your attitude toward others to be my attitude as well. Thank you for the amazing joy that comes from your presence in me!"

by Lisa Cheater

Obedience is a great thing ...

"Children, be obedient to your parents in all things, for this is well-pleasing to the Lord." - **Colossians 3:20**

Teens really struggle with this one. In a time when you are becoming more independent and making bigger decisions, obeying your parents seems like a step backward. Complying makes you feel like a little kid again, but following your parents' rules is so important, that My Father made it one of the Ten Commandments! If you can submit to your earthly mom and dad, then you'll be able to obey Me when you're on your own and life becomes difficult or confusing.

Now What? *Pray:* "Oh God, you know all about my struggles at home. I sometimes think my parents will view me as an adult if I can just make them see things my way. Forgive me for arguing against them when I disagree, for any negative behavior, and for deliberate acts of rebellion. Help me follow godly direction without complaining, today and every day."

Feeling is seeing . . .

"O God, do not remain quiet; Do not be silent and, O God, do not be still." - **Psalms 83:1**

At times, you wonder whether or not I am real. You want evidence, proof of My existence. But, the proof is all around you. You can't see the wind, yet you know it's there because you can feel it and see what it moves. That's the way My Spirit works. I am never still or sleeping. Even if you cannot see Me with your own eyes, you will be able to see the things I do and can feel My presence in your heart. Ask Me to reveal Myself to you today.

Now What? *Pray:* "Yes, Lord, I need a sense of your presence in my life today. Speak to my imagination and reveal yourself today in a way that is undeniably you. Allow me to be sensitive to your subtle voice and your unique ways of reassuring me that you are near. I am listening. I am watching. I am longing for your touch."

by Lisa Cheater

Hang in there ...

"Create in me a clean heart, O God, and renew a steadfast spirit within me." - **Psalms 51:10**

Believing in Me doesn't mean you will suddenly live problem-free. Each day brings its own challenges and joys. That's why I ask you to renew your heart and mind with Me every day. It's easy to become bogged down with cynicism, anger and selfishness, but you can reclaim the zeal you first experienced as a new Believer. Ask for help and forgiveness where you need it and for strength to resist the day's temptations. Let Me recreate you every morning.

Now What? *Pray:* "Jesus, I envision my life like a giant chalkboard full of drawings and thoughts, a record of wrongdoing and hurtful words spoken. The weight and confusion of all that graffiti makes me feel heavy and confused. I want to let it go! Forgive me for these past mistakes. Take your loving hand and wipe away all the sin from my heart so that my life is clean and ready to be filled with your handwriting."

53

Shoe ministry . . .

"Comfort, O comfort My people," says your God." - **Isaiah 40:1**

There is a purpose for everything you are going through. First, you learn and grow in wisdom when you make it through difficulty. And second, struggles allow you to help others. In the future, you will meet other people who are going through the same thing you are now, and you will be able to encourage them because you have walked in their shoes.

Now What? *Pray:* "Thank you for the experiences of my life so far, Lord. The good and the bad have led me to become the person I am now, for the challenges you have allowed me to overcome have made me strong. Place in my path another individual who is going through the same things I have been through so I can encourage them as a witness to your faithfulness."

by Lisa Cheater

Let Me fight your battles …

"Do not be afraid or discouraged because of this vast army. For the battle is not yours, but God's." - **2 Chronicles 20: 15b (NIV)**

I see every problem, every hurdle, and every hurt you endure. As you grow up, more problems will come, and they will be more complicated. But here is the great news: I will come to your aid, every time. Don't be afraid by the size of the challenge before you. Your job is simply to pray and have faith in My will. Fighting the battle is My job!

Now What? *Pray:* "God, I so often find myself thinking, 'No, I can't do this. It's just too hard!' Fear swallows me whole, and I can't seem to move or find my voice. In those times, Lord, help me recall this scripture and to remember that you are here to fight all my battles for me. Give me confidence in your strength, and a willingness to obey."

Garbage in, garbage out . . .

"Finally, brethren, whatever is true, whatever is honorable, whatever is right, whatever is pure, whatever is lovely, whatever is of good repute, if there is any excellence and if anything worthy of praise, dwell on these things." - **Philippians 4:8**

One way Satan gains access into your life is through your thoughts. A mind preoccupied with evil pictures, words, or a defiant attitude is like leaving your backdoor unlocked at night. Keep your thoughts fixed on My righteous words, My sound teaching, and My perfect direction. If you struggle with a particular sin, confess it, and recommit your life to Me right now. Keep that door to your heart locked tight!

Now What? *Pray:* "Jesus, as I go through this day, speak to my mind that I may judge my thoughts and actions according to your ways. Are my actions pure and pleasing to you? Are my words honorable and kind? Do my thoughts bring you joy or shame? Search me, Lord, and mold every fiber of my being into your likeness."

by Lisa Cheater

Kindness is good for you . . .

"The merciful man does himself good, but the cruel man does himself harm." - **Proverbs 11:17**

People who are intentionally cruel to others are miserable all the time. They have no friends, no faith, no hope. They don't realize that kindness rocks! The gratitude of someone you've helped is a precious reward, and just knowing you have made a difference in someone's day is a joyous feeling. People who truly live for Me show it in their actions and in their language. Being merciful keeps you connected to My constant stream of blessing!

Now What? *Pray:* "Lord, I know that following you doesn't mean my life will always be sunshine and roses, but I choose today to be kind to others because it pleases you. I want to be like you even when others choose to be hateful. Grant me the deep peace and blessing that comes from obeying you."

Space and time ...

"My prayer is not for them alone. I pray also for those who <u>will</u> believe in me ..." - **John 17:20 (NIV)**

I prayed for you before you even existed. I asked My Father to bless and protect My followers who were with Me when I walked the Earth, and I asked His help for you, and all those who would believe in Me in the future. I am not bound by time and space, so I can see all that has ever happened, and all that *will* happen, in an instant. I know your future and the plans I have for you. Trust Me. I've been thinking about your life for a very long time.

> Now What? *Pray:* "Father God, you know all about the path before me and how my life will progress. I often wish I could see into the future so I can know what will happen! No doubt there are reasons you allow me to see only the present, and even when I can't see your plan, I will trust and follow you. Lead me in your way, Lord. Close doors I am not meant to walk through, and open others that guide me to your will."

by Lisa Cheater

58

My favorite prayer ...

"When you pray, say: 'Father, hallowed be your name, your kingdom come. Give us each day our daily bread. Forgive us our sins, for we also forgive everyone who sins against us. And lead us not into temptation.'"
- Luke 11:2-4

You don't have to know a bunch of fancy religious words to pray to Me. You don't even have to be in a church. All I need is the sincerest desire of your heart, even if it's a simple, "Lord, help Me." If you don't know where to begin, The Lord's Prayer is a good place. Acknowledge I am God, ask forgiveness for anything you've done wrong, then ask for whatever you need for that day, including protection from overwhelming pressure to sin.

Now What? *Pray:* "Father in Heaven, you are mighty and able to do anything! Thank you for meeting my needs. Keep me away from the evil one, and protect me from temptation. Forgive me for all the sins I'm aware of, those I've forgotten, and give me the strength to forgive others. I love you, Lord."

59

Like you mean it ...

"Therefore I, the prisoner of the Lord, implore you to walk in a manner worthy of the calling with which you have been called, with all humility and gentleness, with patience, showing tolerance for one another in love..." - **Ephesians 4:1-2**

You live in a society that's determined to be right all the time. People argue about the tiniest things just so they can win an argument. This is not how I want you to live. As My follower, you are set above all that pettiness, and you demonstrate your devotion to Me through the way you treat others. Child, you possess the hope that others need to see, so act like it! Be kind and gentle to everyone: your family members, friends, church pals, and, yes, your enemies.

Now What? *Pray:* "Jesus, you are the only perfect example of love in action. It's easy to be nice to nice people, but so hard to be kind to those who are angry and hurtful. Yet that is how you lived. Help me love and pray for those who do not have you in their hearts. Filter my reaction to anger so I can respond with gentleness. I can't do this on my own, Lord. Send your Holy Spirit to fill my thoughts and guide my words."

by Lisa Cheater

60

Never doubt My power...

"I can do all things through Him who strengthens me." - **Philippians 4:13**

Life isn't always easy. Many things seem impossible at first glance, but I will never place you in a situation that you are too weak to bear. The Christian walk is like climbing a tall mountain. Parts of the path appear too steep to manage, but once you push through, the next hill will be easier. I have given you power through My Holy Spirit to do <u>anything</u> if you follow My will.

Now What? *Pray:* "Sometimes I forget, Lord, just how awesome you are. I doubt your power and rely only on my own understanding of a problem. Right now, I am faced with this specific challenge: _____ (name it)____, and at times I feel like abandoning all hope; the task is so difficult. I claim this scripture and acknowledge, that, yes, I *can* do all things with your help! Today, give me courage to keep pressing onward."

Take every thought captive . . .

"Do not complain, brethren, against one another, so that you yourselves may not be judged;" - **James 5:9a**

Every thought that goes through your mind is known to Me (the pleasing ones *and* the not-so-good ones). I know *why* you do the things you do, and that is what I judge most carefully. Even when you make mistakes, I know what is in your heart at the time. So, don't criticize and complain about what your friends are doing. I see them, too. Just keep yourself in check.

Now What? *Pray:* "Jesus, you are the ultimate judge of every heart. Sometimes I get caught up in the need for everything to be fair, and it becomes easy to spot others' faults. Remove my habit of judging others, and forgive me for complaining and harboring resentment in my heart. I will leave judgment to you from this day on."

by Lisa Cheater

I am your gardener ...

"I am the true vine, and My Father is the vinedresser." - **John 15:1**

Have you ever noticed bushes or trees that have been cut back or pruned, sometimes almost to the ground? It may appear harsh, but gardeners do this to help the plant grow thicker and fuller. Like a gardener, I sometimes need to cut away things from your life to help you grow stronger as a Christian. The process can be painful and may seem unfair, but if you trust Me, you'll be so much more productive than you were before.

Now What? *Pray:* "Lord, I confess to you that I don't like being pruned. I don't enjoy having things I deem important removed or having to endure hard times. But I know you are in control and see potential in me to bear lots of spiritual fruit. I will no longer doubt that whatever happens in life is for my best, even if it's hard to accept."

Amazing results . . .

"'If it pleases the king,' [Esther] said, 'and if he regards me with favor and thinks it the right thing to do, and if he is pleased with me, let an order be written overruling the dispatches that Haman ...wrote to destroy the Jews.'" – **Esther 8:5 (NIV)**

Life Situquation #2: Ordinary People + Determination + God's Guidance = Extraordinary Success

Now What? *Pray:* "Father, thank you for Esther's courage to approach her king, speak out against Haman, and save the lives of many Jews! I want that kind of determination and assurance, to stand up for what I know is right. Let me be an example of strength today, just like Esther. Embolden me to avoid going along with the sins of the popular crowd and to speak up for righteousness."

by Lisa Cheater

Be a thermostat not a thermometer . . .

"All the days of the afflicted are bad, but a cheerful heart has a continual feast." - **Proverbs 15:15**

Some people seem always in a dismal funk. Their heads droop, and they have a permanent frown etched on their faces. They choose to reflect the negativity around them and have the amazing ability to bring down an entire group. Don't be one of these gloomy naysayers! You have Me in your heart! Rejoice! Let your joy shine, and look for good, even in tough times. Others will notice your positive disposition, and you will be able to warm up any room with My presence.

Now What? *Pray:* "Yes, Lord, I know people who are always sad like the Pooh character Eeyore. Sometimes, one of those people is me. I am guilty of bringing others down with my attitude. I don't want to be a dark cloud! I desire to be known as the 'person who lights up the room,' and for the expression on my face to match up with the joy in my heart because I have you as my Savior! Help me be a positive influence on others today."

Prayer not revenge . . .

"You shall not take vengeance, nor bear any grudge against the sons of your people, but you shall love your neighbor as yourself; I am the LORD." - **Leviticus 19:18**

Throughout your life, you will encounter people who treat you poorly and others whom you simply don't like. Your first instinct is to retaliate and let your enemy know just exactly what you think of them. When tempted to seek vengeance, though, I ask you to do something difficult: let Me handle your enemies. You are to simply pray for others, treat people the way you want to be treated, and let Me fight the battles. Only then can true justice be served.

Now What? *Pray:* "Lord, no thought is hidden from you, so you already know just how creative I can be when it comes to formulating plans for revenge. But your ways are not like mine, and holding grudges only hurts me. Right now, I need to forgive ____(name them)____ for hurting me, and I leave him/her in your hands. Thank you for fighting my battles and freeing me from hatred."

by Lisa Cheater

Bag complaining . . .

"Do all things without grumbling or disputing so that you will prove yourselves to be blameless and innocent, children of God above reproach in the midst of a crooked and perverse generation, among whom you appear as lights in the world." - **Philippians 2:14-30**

Ouch. No complaining. How come? Grumbling at home shows disrespect to your parents and their authority. Also, people who don't know Me are always looking for a difference in <u>you</u>. As My follower, you are the light of the world, a beacon of hope for others who are lost at school or in the community. If you have the habit of complaining, the lost will not be able to see anything positive about becoming a Christian. By observing your joyfulness, people will realize that I can make a difference in their lives, too!

Now What? *Pray:* "Lord, I see now that complaining is usually about control. I want things to go my way, and when they don't, I am quick to let my opinions fly. Replace my critical attitude with patience, and my need to control situations with total surrender to you. May my faith in you create a positive outlook that will bless those around me."

67

Where's the line?

"But I say to you that everyone who is angry with his brother shall be guilty before the court; and whoever says to his brother, 'You good-for-nothing,' shall be guilty before the supreme court;" - **Matthew 5:22**

It's not enough to simply refrain from punching someone who makes you angry. I say don't even contemplate such an action. Fierce hatred keeps you from enjoying a relationship with Me and goes against My Father's command to love. I know it's hard, especially when you feel you're right, but release those spiteful feelings and replace them with My unconditional love.

Now What? *Pray:* "Jesus, I cannot fathom the love you have for me. I am so imperfect and prone to sin, yet you are steadfast in your love. Always. It is wrong for me to let anger dominate my heart because it prevents me from becoming like you. This moment, I am letting go of any spite and malice I feel toward another person. If I've been wronged, I know you'll handle it, and if I'm at fault, forgive me and help me apologize."

by Lisa Cheater

Life's an open book test...

"Until I come, devote yourself to the public reading of Scripture, to preaching and to teaching." - **1 Timothy 4:13 (NIV)**

I didn't leave you to flounder on earth without a guide or help. The Bible is your immediate source for the answer to any problem you face. Don't confine learning about My Word to Sundays. Each day brings new opportunities for your faith to flourish, but it also brings obstacles that can trip you up if you aren't prepared. Be sure to make time throughout the week to open your Bible and read the things I have to tell you."

Now What? *Pray:* "Lord, why do I worry and wonder so much over the right way to handle an issue? Your Word contains all I need! The next time I encounter a confusing life problem, I will seek guidance first from your scripture instead of calling up my friends or losing sleep about it. Thank you, Jesus, for giving me the Bible as a light for my path."

Keep the lines open . . .

"Pray continually..." - **1 Thessalonians 5:17 (NIV)**

It's that simple. Pray always, all the time. That doesn't mean you have to walk around school or work mumbling to yourself. It means you don't need to wait for church, nighttime, or any other place or hour to talk with me. You don't need the presence of a priest or minister. YOU can talk to Me directly anytime about anything, large or small. When you are in the midst of a test, when you are with a troubled friend, when you have a problem, when you are elated and happy, anytime is a good time to pray.

Now What? *Pray:* "Jesus, you are awesome and amazing! Yes, there are times when I feel so overwhelmed that I want to bury my face and fall to the ground in prayer. But I am so comforted to know that I can simply close my eyes or shift my thoughts to you anyplace, anytime, and you are there. Let me feel your presence close beside me throughout this day."

by Lisa Cheater

The only role model you need . . .

"Fix your eyes on Jesus, the author and perfecter of faith, who for the joy set before Him endured the cross, despising the shame, and has sat down at the right hand of the throne of God." - **Hebrews 12:2**

In this life, you will encounter many people you admire and respect, folks who inspire you by their kindness and goodness. I place these saints in your life as encouragers and teachers, but you have probably learned by now that even the nicest people can let you down. Because humans are fallible and imperfect, you will be disappointed if you look to a certain person as your role model. Look to Me, only, as the perfect example of how to behave in all circumstances. Emulating Me, you will never be disappointed.

Now What? *Pray:* "Lord, you are the only perfect person who has ever walked through the same struggles of life that I face. When others let me down and fall short of my expectations, I will place my faith in you and look to your Word for guidance. Guard my mind from thoughts of failure and prevent me from 'trying on' some other person's mannerisms or personality. You are the one I need to imitate."

Remain pure . . .

"Now flee from youthful lusts and pursue righteousness, faith, love and peace, with those who call on the Lord from a pure heart." - **2 Timothy 2:22**

Marriage isn't something you're concerned about right now, but dating is certainly on your mind. Often. Dating is a pretty serious part of your maturity and not to be taken too casually. It's more than just getting to know someone you like; dating involves learning more about yourself and how to discern the qualities of the one special individual I have already chosen for you. Dear child, don't be fooled by the temporary joy of lust. Take your time and don't settle for anything less than My best for you.

Now What? *Pray:* "Lord Jesus, it's hard to imagine that you already know all about my future spouse! It may be someone I haven't even met yet, but as I commit to remain pure until I meet this person, I ask that you also keep him/her pure as well. Teach my future spouse to be kind, loving, and righteous so that when we meet, I will know without a doubt it's a match made in Heaven."

by Lisa Cheater

Would you want YOU as a friend?

"Treat others the same way you want them to treat you." - **Luke 6:31**

Should you call, or should you text? Should you yell or act cool? Should you apologize or ignore? Relationships can be very complicated, but if you remember this scripture from Luke, you will always do the right thing. You live in a world that is dominated by selfish desires, so placing yourself in someone else's position can be difficult. But try. Instead of protecting your own self interests today, look at things through another person's point of view, then treat them the way you'd want to be treated.

Now What? *Pray:* "Lord, I know I clash most with _____(name person)_____. I want this individual to see things my way. I want to be right. Help me put myself in their place. How would I want to be treated if I were this person? It takes so much courage for me to act on the answer to that question, but I know you will help me. Even if he/she rejects my attempt to do the right thing, at least I know I have pleased you."

73

Practice patience . . .

"Therefore be patient, brethren, until the coming of the Lord. The farmer waits for the precious produce of the soil, being patient about it, until it gets the early and late rains." - **James 5:7**

It would be absurd for a farmer to stand over a newly planted seed and demand that it produce a tomato by the next day or else! He knows the seed needs time to warm, germinate, sprout, receive water and nutrients, and grow before it can bear fruit. Complaining about it would be pointless. Patience is waiting *without* complaining. Some situations in life will not bend to your need for instant gratification. In those times where you must endure waiting, let Me sustain you with self-control and understanding.

Now What? *Pray:* "Jesus, yes, there are many times when I complain about situations over which I have no control. Arguing seems to only make things worse, and yet it's so tough for me to reign in my negative attitude and defiant remarks. Give me patience when I must wait, and help me resist the urge to bicker and fight when I want things sooner. Thank you, Lord, for evidence of your careful handiwork in my life."

by Lisa Cheater

74

The company you keep...

"Walk with the wise and become wise, for a companion of fools suffers harm." - **Proverbs 13:20 (NIV)**

Who are your friends? Do you spend your time with people who are growing Christians, like you, that uplift and help you be your best, or do you hang with fools who are consistently in trouble? Yes, you are to pray for the lost and reach out to non-Believers so that they may see Me in you, but your closest friends, the ones you rely upon, should be of strong character. You are not being judgmental when you choose wise and thoughtful people to be your friends. They are my gifts of help and support.

Now What? *Pray:* "Lord, thank you for being the best friend I will ever have. You are always here to love and support me no matter what. I can't say that about all my earthly friends. Help me to see which of my relationships are not helpful to my Christian walk, and give me the courage to respectfully dissolve those damaging associations. Fill my path with people who are Believers, who love you, and have the capacity to love and strengthen me."

Creation is not a theory . . .

"In the beginning God created the Heavens and the earth." -
Genesis 1:1

Science is finally beginning to point to the truth of creation.
Most agree that a specific historical event occurred from which the
planets and stars were formed, but man can no longer deny the incredibly
small margin of error that allows life to exist on earth. If one planet's
moon went off course, life would cease. It's no accident. God the Father
holds all of creation in His hand and knows exactly how much gravity,
atmospheric oxygen, and warmth is required for earth to sustain life.
Look into the construction of the universe and you will find God's
fingerprint.

> *Now What?* *Pray:* "Lord, I do not understand all the
> inner workings of the universe, but I am confident that you
> have made it perfectly. The beauty of creation reminds
> me of your love. I see your majesty in the mountains, your
> strength in the ocean, and your vastness along the beaches.
> One day I will see your creation as you see it, but for now,
> I am content to know you are in control. Thank you for life
> and all the joy within it."

by Lisa Cheater

No hammers necessary...

"Blessed are the peacemakers, for they shall be called sons of God." -
Matthew 5:9

I adore peacemakers, people who are always looking out for what is right and good according to My Father's will. Though the world is full of people who love to stir up trouble, Christians should rejoice in peacefulness and order. Don't become like those who seem determined to create conflict with everyone. Demonstrate your strength through self-control.

Now What? *Pray:* "Jesus, though I long for stability and contentment, I know that I am often not an instrument of peace. I find myself angry over small things, moody when I should be happy, and complaining when I should be looking for solutions to problems. Help me, Lord, to learn from your example so I can be a peacemaker, too."

77

Day 77

All arms?

"For just as we have many members in one body and all the members do not have the same function, so we, who are many, are one body in Christ, and individually members one of another." - **Romans 12:4-5**

Each Believer has a specific gift from the Holy Spirit: some are wonderful teachers, some can sing, paint, write, or preach. Some are outgoing, others are quiet. Just as your body would cease to function without all its different parts, so would My body, the church. All skills and personalities are important to help My church function. One is not more important than the other! I need you and your specific gifts, exactly as I intended!

> Now What? *Pray:* "Lord, thank you for the way you've created me. You have given me very specific abilities such as : ____(name them)____, gifts you intend for me to bring you glory and encourage others. Forgive me for feeling jealous towards others who have cool talents that I want, and, instead, may I seek to become the best 'me' I can be."

by Lisa Cheater

Complete teaching ...

"I have filled him with the Spirit of God in wisdom, in understanding, in knowledge, and in all kinds of craftsmanship." - **Exodus 31:3**

Tests are huge part of your life right now. I know it seems as if you are always preparing for some kind of exam in school that measures how much you've learned, but your faith is also frequently tested by Satan. Sometimes I allow those tests to strengthen and teach you about My ways, and sometimes I protect you from difficulties I know you cannot yet handle. Rest assured, I provide all the knowledge you need for any kind of testing, whether at school, in life, or in developing your gifts. Seek Me for clarity and comprehension, be diligent in studying, and remain focused as you prepare for academic and life tests. I will give you the answers."

> Now What? *Pray:* "Jesus, I realize that my test anxiety is often caused by my own lack of preparation. In school, keep me focused and calm, grant me understanding of difficult subjects, and help me prioritize my time to include adequate study. In life, help me stay focused on the wisdom and teachings of your Word, prompt me to learn and remember scriptures so that whenever I am tested, I'll be ready. Thank you, Jesus, for caring about me so completely."

Spring will come ...

"There is an appointed time for everything. And there is a time for every event under Heaven." - **Ecclesiastes 3:1**

Some days it seems nothing goes right. Everything you touch falls apart, and you can't see when or how things will get better. Those times can feel like the season of winter: bleak, miserable, cold, and depressing. But you cannot completely appreciate spring and summer without first going through winter! The difficult times in your life make the happy times so much more joyous! Your problems *will* pass into a season of spring.

Now What? *Pray:* "Father, protect me during the winter seasons in my life, when everything I touch seems to fail, when I feel depressed or alone. Wrap me in your loving arms and remind me that you are present in every circumstance. Nothing touches me that hasn't first filtered through your hands. Thank you, Lord, for your encouragement to make it through life's darkest times."

by Lisa Cheater

I get where you're coming from . . .

"Then Judas Iscariot, who was one of the twelve, went off to the chief priests in order to betray Him to them." - **Mark 14:10**

I know firsthand how it feels to have a friend betray you. The words and actions of some of My closest friends cut through Me deeper than the flogger's whip. Although I was truly afraid the night before My crucifixion, I chose to forgive those who had wronged Me. I came to earth to teach, but to also experience every emotion that you feel. Trust Me. I understand what it's like to be human.

Now What? *Pray:* "Lord Jesus, thank you for entering history two thousand years ago just so you could relate to me. I forget that although you are God, you were also a man and saw the world with human eyes for a short while. You were loved, heralded, then mistreated, mocked, murdered, and buried. Yet you won by rising from death, and I know you will never betray me! Thank you for your faithfulness."

Balm for the soul . . .

"Pleasant words are a honeycomb, sweet to the soul and healing to the bones." - **Proverbs 16:24**

As spring blooms, bees will begin their natural search for all things pollen. All day, certain bee species will search for the key ingredient in making their life's treasure: honey. Imagine words with the effect of honey. Soothing, sweet, delightful, gentle. It's impossible to feel angst or bitterness when using kind speech. When negative thoughts invade your mind, replace them with words of honey. When you encounter the harsh words of an angry person, respond with words of honey. Those in need of encouragement will be drawn to you just like bees to a hive.

Now What? *Pray:* "Father, I have a choice every time I speak. Will I add fuel to the fire of an argument or will I extinguish anger with sweet words of honey? I know which choice you desire. Lord, give me your words, and speak through me when my human side wants to lash out with damaging speech. Fill me with your spirit so that my language is an overflow of my love for you."

by Lisa Cheater

Finish what you start . . .

"...Persevere in these things, for as you do this you will ensure salvation both for yourself and for those who hear you." - **1 Timothy 4:16**

How do you want to be known at school? As a reliable and confident leader, or as one who is undependable and follows the crowd? When your goals seem far off and unattainable, remember that many people are counting on you. Some may come to know Me because of your example and persistence! Guard your reputation by keeping your promises and honoring your commitments.

Now What? *Pray:* "Father God, there are times when I feel like quitting activities, projects, sports, and quests because they become hard or I'm afraid of failure. I can't see the light at the end of the tunnel. Help me maintain strong character, to be diligent in finishing the things I start. Most of all, Jesus, thank you for never giving up on me."

83

Respect your leaders ... even the crabby ones.

"Servants, be submissive to your masters with all respect, not only to those who are good and gentle, but also to those who are unreasonable."-
1 Peter 2:18

Once there was a young Army private who totally hated his commanding officer. The officer was a strict perfectionist, and made his men run drills in the rain and in the middle of the night. Two years later, this platoon was the only one to survive a vicious battle in a remote jungle—all because of the skills they'd learned from that hard-driving sergeant.

Authorities are placed in your path by Me. Show them respect by obeying rules, even if you disagree.

> Now What? *Pray:* "Lord, I accept your authority by accepting the leadership of those you place over me: my parents, teachers, church leaders, government officials... these people are here to instruct and guide me, and I will respect them with my attitude and obedience. I lift up those leaders who may not know you as their Savior, that they will begin to seek a relationship with you as their ultimate authority."

by Lisa Cheater

Golden silence . . .

"But Jesus Himself would often slip away to the wilderness and pray."-
Luke 5:16

I created you to work, play, and rest. Even I took time out of teaching to pray and rest up for what the Father had planned for Me. If you are always running on empty—little sleep, too much food, not enough food, little exercise—you won't have the mojo to do your best at school, help others, or fight illness. Take care of yourself and spend time just being quiet and listening to Me. (BTW, that means turning off your cell phone and iPod®, and heading to a quiet place where you won't be interrupted or sidetracked.)

Now What? *Pray:* "Lord, I know I don't take care of myself as I should. I don't realize how much noise is in my life until I turn it all off. Show me ways to schedule healthy, productive downtime, restful periods that allow me to grow in my faith and restore my body. Give me the desire to study your Word and communicate in quiet with you. Thank you for creating this gift of rest."

Show mercy . . .

"Blessed are the merciful, for they shall receive mercy." - **Matthew 5:7**

If you expect Me to bless you with mercy, you must also show mercy to others. Living for Me often means behaving in a way that is contrary to the world. That includes forgiving others, releasing grudges, helping the poor or those who are hurting, and avoiding gossip. You won't be perfect at it, but I'm asking you to try with My help.

> Now What? *Pray:* "Lord, give me your heart of mercy and the discipline to demonstrate love by helping others, even those I feel don't deserve my assistance. This is so contrary to my normal thinking that it will require your supernatural control of my thoughts and behavior! Today, open my eyes to see those in need, as you see them, and to love them just as you love me."

by Lisa Cheater

Love your enemy . . .

"I say to you, love your enemies and pray for those who persecute you..." - **Matthew 5:44**

That one hurts doesn't it? It's so hard to love or pray for people who treat you bad. Nevertheless, that's one thing that separates Christians from non-Believers. If you love Me more than anything, you'll pray for the classmate who teases you, the teacher who harps on you, the neighbor who is selfish, and the sibling who changes the TV channel on you without asking. Amazing changes will take place in your heart, and maybe theirs, too.

Now What? *Pray:* "Jesus, I realize that I fall short of this commandment. Forgive me for ignoring or retaliating against the people I don't like for they are the very ones who need you most. I ask for you to touch my enemies, to soften their hearts, and to repair relationships where necessary. Help me remember to pray for my enemies instead of fighting."

Instant access . . .

"I have hidden your word in my heart that I might not sin against you."-
Psalms 119:11 (NIV)

Hiding My Word in your heart doesn't mean you keep your love for Me a secret. It means memorizing specific scripture verses so when you are faced with a difficulty or challenge, you'll know what to do. Locking scriptures in your mind allows you to access them at any time. Instead of listening to the lies of Satan, you will be able to recall the promises of God. The Truth of the Word is like a mighty sword that slices though any of the enemy's tricks. Choose this verse or another to commit to memory today.

Now What? *Pray:* "Jesus I want to build up my arsenal of memorized scriptures so I will have the tools to flee from temptation and sin every day. Help me hide your Word in my heart so that I will not sin against you. Bring to mind other scriptures that I find meaningful, and embed them permanently into my memory. Thank you, Lord, for the incredible power of your living Word!"

by Lisa Cheater

88

Free to choose . . .

"For what I do is not the good I want to do; no, the evil I do not want to do--this I keep on doing." - **Romans 7:19 (NIV)**

The apostle Paul said these words above. He was one of My best leaders, and even *he* struggled with following My teaching! Humankind will always battle against its sinful nature, but I give you the ability to *choose* right. I don't want you to be a mindless Jesus Zombie! You are free to love Me, but I will not force you to do so; love stops being love when it is required. Don't beat yourself up when you feel like you are struggling to do what is right. Trust my plan as you grow and mature.

Now What? *Pray:* "Lord, I constantly feel the pull of emotions and hormones, disappointment and joy, elation and depression, calmness and frantic desperation. At times I think I'm going nuts! I can chalk up part of my struggle to adolescence, but I am so glad to know that I am not alone, that all people battle against sin. I am not a loser—I am learning! Help me choose you every day, in every situation."

Will you stand up for me?

"Now Peter was sitting outside in the courtyard, and a servant-girl came to him and said, 'You too were with Jesus the Galilean.' But he denied it before them all, saying, 'I do not know what you are talking about.'" - **Matthew 26:69-70**

My disciple Peter promised he'd never turn his back on Me, but when I was arrested, he claimed he didn't know Me at all because he was afraid he'd get in trouble, too. Would you admit to being a Christian if confronted? Or would you downplay your faith in order to look cool? When someone asks you about your faith, stand firm and say, "Yes, I am a follower of Jesus!" Your courage will grant you favor with God.

Now What? *Pray:* "Wow. I let you down alot, Jesus. I am surrounded by people who curse your name, and I fail to speak up when I see people hurting or insulting another individual. Forgive me for keeping my light hidden. Replace my fear of rejection and embarrassment with a boldness for you! Today I will surely be put to this test. Prick my heart and give me courage to prove that you are my Lord."

by Lisa Cheater

God's ways don't always make sense . . .

"And Jesus prayed 'Abba! Father! All things are possible for You; remove this cup from Me; yet not what I will, but what You will.'" - **Mark 14:36**

I didn't eagerly and happily follow the path to the cross. I knew what was coming and it was terrifying. I asked My Father to get Me out of it, but I knew that wasn't His will. If he had rescued Me, there'd be no Christianity, no Salvation, no direct bridge between sinful people and a holy God. That's why, at the moment of My death, the veil that separated the holy section of the temple from the people was torn in half. It was a symbol of God's love and a promise that nothing would ever separate Him from His people again.

Now What? *Pray:* "God, help me accept your will especially when I can't see how you are working in my life. When things seem to be going my way, I have no trouble giving you credit, but when life seems to be fighting against me, I am quick to give you the blame. Grant me peace in times of struggle. Even when my plans fail, I will trust in you for I know you love me and are working for my good behind the scenes."

91

Today, be wise . . .

"A fool finds pleasure in evil conduct, but a man of understanding delights in wisdom." - **Proverbs 10:23 (NIV)**

Are you a fool or wise? A fool is someone who is easily tricked and enjoys breaking the rules. Not cool. My great plans for your life can only happen if you *choose* to be wise. Who do you consider wise? Think of a person you respect, one who seems joyful and in control of his or her behavior. What about them makes them admirable? When in doubt, here's a simple, well-used litmus test: the next time you are tempted to do something foolish, just ask yourself, "What would Jesus do?"

Now What? *Pray:* "Jesus, next to you, the person I most admire and respect is ____(name them)____. They have your qualities and joy, and others are drawn to this person because of their godly personality. I want to have an impact for your kingdom through my presence and attitude, not to be like this person, but to be more like *you*. Empty me of any unrighteousness and plant your spirit in my heart. May those I come in contact with see you in me every day."

by Lisa Cheater

See love in the cross ...

"For God so loved the world, that He gave His only begotten Son, that whoever believes in Him shall not perish, but have eternal life." - **John 3:16**

You probably know this verse by heart, but I want you to really consider what it says. My Father loved you so much that He made a permanent way for you to be free from sin: My death on the cross. I was the ultimate sacrifice. You don't ever have to say, "I'm a mess! It's just the way I was born." You were born to achieve mighty things, to be loved by Me, and to love others. Claim that blessing today!

Now What? *Pray:* "Jesus, thank you for giving your life for me on the cross. I cannot imagine the depth of love you have for me! So often my failures and problems cover me like an avalanche, and I find it hard to face you, afraid that I'm not good enough to ask your forgiveness. Give me the courage to seek you when I don't feel worthy and the faith I need to believe that your love can cover all my sin."

The greatest day . . .

"Every knee shall bow to Me, and every tongue shall give praise to God." - **Romans 14:11**

Why do you spend so much time rebelling against My truth? You wonder if I am real, if all those Bible stories of amazing miracles actually took place, and if live in a perfect place called Heaven. The answer is yes! Although many around you choose to turn away from Me, one day, every person in the entire world will bow down to Me. All will know that you were right to follow Me, the REAL King!

Now What? *Pray:* "Lord, I long for the day when everyone around the world will finally realize YOU are the only path to Heaven! What an awesome day that will be! Thank you for saving me and for adopting me into your family. Who can I tell about you? Place the name of a person on my heart who does not have a relationship with you. Grant me the courage to speak boldly of my faith with my friends so that they may experience the joy of your return with me!"

by Lisa Cheater

94

Forgive others . . .

"For if you forgive others for their transgressions, your Heavenly Father will also forgive you. But if you do not forgive others, then your Father will not forgive your transgressions." - **Matthew 6:14-15**

It is your natural inclination to hold a grudge against unlovable people. You may even feel completely justified in your hatred. After all, what's to love about a bully, a racist, or a drama queen? Remember, they are my creations, just like you. Although you might never strike back at someone who wrongs you, I ask you to go a step further and actually forgive them. You aren't perfect either, and God forgives you whenever you repent. Do the same.

Now What? *Pray:* "Father God, I know my actions and behavior are imperfect; I need your forgiveness every day! I understand that in order to receive your full mercy, I must first forgive others. At this moment, a person I need to forgive is: ____(name them)____. I lay my bitterness toward them at the foot of your cross. Cleanse my heart of resentment. With your help, I will avoid gossiping and complaining about this person to others from this day forward."

95

It's all just stuff...

"Do not store up for yourselves treasures on earth, where moth and rust destroy, and where thieves break in and steal. But store up for yourselves treasures in Heaven..." - **Matthew 6:19-20**

Cell phones, the best clothes, computers, games, cars, jaw-dropping sneakers, a cool room, the newest iPod...they're things you think about all the time, things that make you feel good. For a while. None of these things will be useful 100 years from now. They'll stop working or simply wear out. But the things you do for Me will last forever! My love can never be stolen and never needs charging! In fact, it grows stronger over time, and the feelings you experience by obeying my commands are worth far more than jewels and gold.

Now What? *Pray:* "Jesus, I confess that I do love certain material objects, especially: ____(name it)____. But I also recognize that the high I feel from obtaining these things is temporary. I want to store up treasures in Heaven by actively doing things here on earth that grow your kingdom! Help me speak kindly, assist others in need, give to those who don't have enough, and tell people about your love. Thank you, Lord, for all the blessings you have showered upon me!"

by Lisa Cheater

Tried and true . . .

"As for God, His way is blameless; The word of the LORD is tried; He is a shield to all who take refuge in Him." - **Psalms 18:30**

You have been on the earth for such a short time, and yet you often question My power. You forget that I have been around since the beginning of time itself, and for thousands of years men have tried to prove that My way is faulty, that My Word is unreliable. They could not. Because I am full of Truth and Light, no other religion, philosophy, self-talk, or individual can stand up against Me. I am the same today as I was in the beginning of time, and My love-centered teaching will endure throughout eternity.

Now What? *Pray:* "Lord Jesus, no other person deserves my praise, for only you created the universe, personally invaded history to walk with us, suffered faithfully for our iniquities, then defeated sin and death by rising from the grave! I am overwhelmed to think about your incredible power! Keep me steadfast and true to you alone, Father, and protect my wandering mind from any false teaching."

Be careful not to judge . . .

"Why do you look at the speck that is in your brother's eye, but do not notice the log that is in your own eye?" - **Matthew 7:3**

It's so simple to pick out someone else's faults. You can easily pinpoint all the things your friends do wrong and wonder why they can't see it for themselves. Beware pious accusations, for when you point a finger at someone, three fingers point back at you! You might even be guilty of doing the exact things you are quick to point out in others. Instead of judging, spend time thinking about and correcting your own behavior.

Now What? *Pray:* "God, place a mirror before me and help me see my own behavior as you see it. Have I been hypocritical? Do I criticize others about actions for which I am also guilty? Forgive me, Lord, for failing to see my own sin. Convict my heart of anything I have done against you or others. Today, prevent me from complaining about or verbally judging anyone."

by Lisa Cheater

Can I be a rock star?

"Delight yourself in the LORD; and He will give you the desires of your heart." - **Psalms 37:4**

No, this promise doesn't mean that I will suddenly turn you into a film star and set you up with Justin Bieber or Taylor Swift. It means that if you are trying to follow My teachings daily and spending time with Me in prayer, I will help you do whatever you need to do. If you need to pass a test, I'll give you the wisdom to know how to study. If you long for a relationship, I will give you joy and peace that fills that longing until the time is right. Need money? I'll help you manage what you have and give you insight about ways to increase it. How? It's all in scripture and in the words that I give your church leaders and parents to speak to you. Listen to them!

Now what? *Pray:* "Jesus, clear away any muck between us, so that I am fully committed to serving you and able to give you complete control over my life. The thing I most desire right now is:_____(name it)_____. Is this part of your vision for me or a creation of my own selfish desires? Reveal scriptures to me that bring clarity to my goals and strengthen me to abandon frivolous wishes. Grant me peace while I wait."

99

Non-exclusive club . . .

"The angel said to them, 'Do not be afraid; for behold, I bring you good news of great joy which will be for all the people;'" - **Luke 2:9-10**

I came into the world for everyone, not just a few groups of people. My love isn't limited to any one culture or race; I am the Savior of all who believe in Me. There's no need for you to try on different religions as you get older. I am The Way. I died for you and every person you will lay eyes upon today: the poor, the sick, the kind, the criminal, the wealthy, the underdog, the popular, the drug addict, the alcoholic...*everyone.*

> Now What? *Pray:* "Lord, I am often confronted with information about other religions in school, at church, and from friends. Sometimes I wonder if we all worship the same god and just call you by different names, but I know that is a lie from the enemy meant to confuse me. You are the only way to Heaven and salvation! Prevent me from being confused or seduced by other religions. Instead, I ask for your spirit to be revealed to these people, that they may understand you died for them, too."

by Lisa Cheater

Shine like the sun . . .

"Then the righteous will shine forth as the sun in the kingdom of their Father." - **Matthew 13:43**

Remember the last time it rained for several days in a row? The whole earth seemed gloomy and miserable. When the sun returned, you were so relieved! It warmed your face and made you want to linger outside. To the world, Christians should be like those welcome, warming rays of sunlight. Through your smile and joy, let My presence fill up and brighten any space.

> Now What? *Pray:* "Father, God, just as we are drawn outside into the warmth of the sun, I want my life to be an example of hope for those who do not know you as their Savior. Yet I can only be a shining light if I let you live completely in me. Instead of reflecting the sadness and darkness around me, allow me to brighten the lives of those I come in contact with. Suppress my selfishness so that others clearly see your character in my behavior."

101

The best leaders are servants . . .

"The one who is the greatest among you must become like the youngest, and the leader like the servant." - **Luke 22:26**

In action movies, leaders are usually the big tough guys, the ones who tell others what to do. In My eyes, great leadership means more than being able to organize and motivate people. It means you are willing to serve others at the same time. Wouldn't you rather follow a leader who respects and cares for you? Look for opportunities today to be a servant leader.

Now What? *Pray:* "Lord, you are the perfect example of servant leadership. You respectfully and lovingly led the disciples and new followers by meeting their physical and spiritual needs. Show me how I can lead others by serving them. Push away my prideful longing to be praised, and give me the opportunity to gain respect by selflessly helping those in need. Just as you did."

by Lisa Cheater

Inside out . . .

"Be devoted to one another in brotherly love; give preference to one another in honor; not lagging behind in diligence, fervent in spirit, serving the Lord; rejoicing in hope, persevering in tribulation, devoted to prayer..." - **Romans 12:10-12**

This directive goes against everything we know about teens who are often self-centered, moody, dramatic, angry, and grumpy when they haven't been fed. Who would want such a critter?! ME! Adolescence is riddled with angst and hormones that are part of the way I created your body to grow. Learning to shed those selfish tendencies is how I intend for your character and spirit to mature! Be joyful during this time! You are evolving into a meaningful warrior for God's Kingdom!

Now What? *Pray:* "Lord, sometimes I feel so many conflicting emotions that I long to be older, to bypass adolescence all together and get on with adulthood! But just as a butterfly benefits from its lone struggle out of a cocoon, I must press on through this phase of my life with courage and faith in your grand design for my life. Make my heart soft in order to more easily learn the lessons before me, and guard my mind against rebellion that leads to trouble. I trust you, Jesus."

Do unto others...

"In everything, therefore, treat people the same way you want them to treat you." - **Matthew 7:12**

You don't like being bullied, yelled at, and pushed around, so don't do it to others. Act the way you want people to behave toward you: patient, kind, gentle, enthusiastic, thoughtful, loving. These aren't just nice personality traits. They are the fruits of My spirit! Live as an example of how you want to be treated.

Now What? *Pray:* "Lord, sometimes the only way I think I can communicate my true feelings is to act them out. I brood, pout, scream, cry, sass, withdraw... behaviors that only make me feel worse and push away the people I love. The world cannot see you in me when I act like that, so help me treat others respectfully and encourage them when they need it."

by Lisa Cheater

I am always in control ...

"I know that You can do all things, and that no purpose of Yours can be thwarted." - **Job 42:2**

At times the whole world feels completely out of control, like a ship without a captain. Wars, natural disasters, and hatred make life appear as though evil is winning over Me. Rest assured My plans are never ruined, and I am never surprised or taken off-guard by the deeds of others. My goals for you will be fulfilled even if you (and others) make mistakes from time to time.

Now What? *Pray:* "Father, God, yes, at times, it does seem like the world is falling apart; there is so much evil! But you are always in control, and each day you are shaping me into the person you need me to be. Through difficulties and heartbreak, I will trust you with my life. Strengthen my faith in your purposes so I will not become discouraged, and help me accept my mistakes and learn from them."

105

Fame isn't "all that"...

"He who loves money will not be satisfied with money..." - **Ecclesiastes 5:10**

In the news today there are stories of celebrities who have lost their way in pursuit of their dreams, venturing into excess, drugs, and sex. They have every material extravagance, and yet it's never enough because they don't know Me. Many assume that money and fame will fill a hole in their hearts, but that hole is God-shaped. Nothing else will satisfy. Don't rely on money, people, or possessions to make you happy. Only I can bring real, lasting peace and gladness.

Now What? *Pray:* "Lord, I confess I am often jealous of what others have. The shine, the speed, and the flair all tempt me to envy. Thank you for the things you have given me thus far, and prevent me from being drawn into the temptation to covet material possessions, for that road leads to disappointment and regret. I will turn my longings to you, Lord. Your path leads to unspeakable joy."

by Lisa Cheater

You are My weapon . . .

"He made me into a polished arrow and concealed me in his quiver."-
Isaiah 49:2 (NIV)

A quiver is a bag of arrows that a warrior carries on his back. To be ready for a battle, each arrow must be polished and ready, and the process of making strong, straight arrows is brutal. The metal is heated, hammered, and ground against stone. Difficulties you encounter are like that polishing stone; the grind may be unpleasant, but it can make you very strong. If you weather the process with Me, you will become a mighty weapon against evil!

> Now What? *Pray:* "Lord, thank you for choosing me to be a part of your Kingdom's quiver. You do not send hardships to break me down, but, rather, allow them to build me up. It's hard for me to imagine myself as a mighty warrior or a weapon in your armory, but I will try to embrace life's challenges as steps in the process of sharpening my character. I am yours, Lord, and in you I place my trust."

Rejoice in insults . . .

"Blessed are you when people insult you and persecute you, and falsely say all kinds of evil against you because of Me." - **Matthew 5:11**

Don't expect non-Christians to act like Christians! It isn't possible. People who are not connected to Me have no idea what you're talking about when you speak to them about having a "relationship with Christ." They may even cover up their confusion by making fun of you or saying hurtful things. Don't be upset! You may have planted a seed in their mind that will someday cause them to seek Me. For that, I call you blessed!

Now What? *Pray:* "Jesus, the last thing I feel when people say hurtful things about me is blessed! Malicious rumors and humiliation cut me to the very core. Yet I realize these words come from the master of all lies, Satan, in an attempt to chip away at my faith and strength in you. O Lord, I will not let mere words break me down because you are stronger! Guard my heart against verbal attacks, and help me recognize truthful words versus words of deceit."

by Lisa Cheater

Remember ...

"...and when He had given thanks, He broke it and said, 'This is My body, which is for you; do this in remembrance of Me.'" - **1 Corinthians 11:24**

You celebrate your birthday with a lovely cake each year. It's a sweet reminder of your birth, your special day, and you're always eager to pause to make a special wish before blowing out the candles. Think of Me every day, but every time communion, the Lord's Supper, comes before you, be sure to pause and remember My special sacrifice and how the Father always delivers on His promises. Before you eat take the bread and cup, pray for a fresh commitment to Me. Your devotion will bless you more than any wish.

Now What? *Pray:* "Jesus, I thank you today for the sacrifice you made on the cross, for giving up your life to pay the debt of my sins. I cannot repay the price you paid, but I can give you my life. This day, I recommit my will, my dreams, my plans, my thoughts, my speech, my actions, and my talents to you. You are so gracious to bring good out of my life. Use me for your glory."

It's okay to do nothing ...

"Remember the Sabbath day, to keep it holy." - **Exodus 20:8**

You are so busy throughout the week, it's tough to catch up with you! Activities, television, friends, school, church, the phone, computers, iPods, games...your world is so full of noise and distraction, it's no wonder you're exhausted most of the time! I have laid aside a day of rest you, the Sabbath, in the Ten Commandments for you to relax, restore and rejuvenate. Don't push aside this gift! Take Sunday to listen to Me, to rest, and renew your strength.

Now What? *Pray:* "Father, thank you for your provision of rest and quiet in the Sabbath. Many people treat Sunday like a second Saturday (myself included), but I want to honor this special day by taking a break from usual busy work and reflecting on you. I'm so used to being busy that being still seems like a guilty pleasure! Teach me to use this time to replenish my spiritual and physical strength for the crazy week ahead."

by Lisa Cheater

110

Problems are a guarantee ...

"In this world you will have trouble. But take heart! I have overcome the world."- **John 16:33 (NIV)**

Why do you let complications bring you down as though you have no hope? Though your life will never be 100% free from hard times and problems, never forget that I overcame the grave, and I can overcome your most challenging difficulties, too. These temporary troubles are opportunities for you to grow in wisdom. Place your trust in Me, pray, and study My Word. I will give you comfort and direction in the midst of your trouble. Guaranteed.

Now What? *Pray:* "Yes, Jesus, you overcame the grave and sin, and you alone are mighty enough to help me overcome my fears, disappointments, and hurts. Prevent hopelessness from ever taking root in my mind. With you, I am a conqueror. With you, I am unshakable. With you, I am mighty! With you, I am able to stand through the toughest trials. Thank you, Lord Jesus, for your encouragement, for lifting me to my feet once again."

Hypocrite? Don't be one!

"But among you there must not be even a hint of sexual immorality, or of any kind of impurity, or of greed, because these are improper for God's holy people." - **Ephesians 5:3 (NIV)**

A hypocrite is a person who says he believes one thing and acts completely opposite. There are many examples of well-known Christian leaders who have fallen to temptation and gotten caught, often by cameras or email! Non-Believers argue there's no reason to follow Me because Christians don't act any different than the rest of the world. Prove them wrong! Make sure your behavior is blameless before of all people.

Now What? *Pray:* "Lord, I'm not certain my casual acquaintances would be able to tell I am a Christian by the way I behave and talk. I'm often inconsistent, behaving one way at church, another way at home or at school. Search me, Lord, and see if there is evidence of hypocrisy in my life. Remove it, Jesus, so that the love I have for you is reflected in my actions every day, no matter where I am."

by Lisa Cheater

112

All exposed...

"Are not two sparrows sold for a cent? And yet not one of them will fall to the ground apart from your Father." - **Matthew 10:29**

You have no idea how much I love you. God, My Father, knows when one tiny bird dies in the forest and when you shed one single tear. You are My beloved, worth much more to Me than anything else in creation. I *want* to help when you are hurting, when you are troubled, or in a mess. You can confide in Me because I care so much about you.

Now What? *Pray:* "God, you seem too big to know about the tiniest details of my life, and yet that's exactly what your Word claims. I may be able to hide my secret thoughts and fears from other people, but not from you. And you love me still. Help me remember that I am worthy. I am precious. Thank you, Lord, for your never-ending love."

Truly satisfied . . .

"Blessed are you who hunger now, for you shall be satisfied." -
Luke 6:21

Way too much of your favorite candy, the hippest clothes
and fad bracelets, a new iPod, drugs, sex before marriage... these are
just some of the things young people think will make them feel good
about themselves. Instead of filling the voids in your life with trinkets
and addictions, focus your attention on the joy that only comes from
following Me. Push aside that Snicker's, and let Me satisfy your longing
for happiness and acceptance (with zero calories and no trans fat).

> Now What? *Pray:* "Jesus, I have tried a few shortcuts
> to happiness, and they have all failed. I can be easily
> enticed by things of this world and the empty promises
> of smooth-sounding words, so help me see these are
> merely the enemy's tools for temptation. Keep my eyes
> focused on your will for me and let me hunger only for
> your Truth."

by Lisa Cheater

Would you die for a friend?

"For God did not send the Son into the world to judge the world, but that the world might be saved through Him." - **John 3:17**

I didn't die on the cross to become a martyr. I willingly gave My life in order to pay the ultimate sacrifice for the sins of the entire world. For YOUR sins. I came not to tell you what you're doing wrong, but to free you from the need to sin, to give you a better, alternate way of responding to temptation. I am not your dictator; I am your Deliverer!

Now What? *Pray:* "Jesus, thank you for dying for my sins on the cross. I want to be free from the daily burdens that weigh down my spirit, and so I confess them to you now. You have brought to mind these things I have done wrong: ____(name them)____. Lord, forgive me, and bring me back into your close care. I freely offer you my heart and life completely, Lord. Thank you for rescuing us from the pain of sin and guilt!"

Sin TKO...

"For the flesh sets its desire against the Spirit, and the Spirit against the flesh; for these are in opposition to one another..." - **Galatians 5:17**

You often feel as though there is some kind of war raging inside you (besides hormones.) Your human nature wants to sin and get away with it. My Spirit, which is also in you, wants you to stick to what you learn from the Bible and My teachings. These two forces are constantly fighting like a WWF take-down match! Don't be distraught over this battle. Let My Holy Spirit win by resisting the temptations of your desires. The more you practice giving Me control, the easier it will become.

Now What? *Pray:* "Yes, Lord, so much about being a teen involves a battle for control. I'm learning to become self-reliant and dependent upon you at the same time, and it's often very confusing! As my parents give me more responsibility, teach me to rely upon you for direction and guidance. My parents won't always be around me, but you will always be here to keep me on track."

by Lisa Cheater

Crystal ball . . .

"'For I know the plans I have for you,' declares the LORD, 'plans to prosper you and not to harm you, plans to give you hope and a future.'"- **Jeremiah 29:11 (NIV)**

Do you read those horoscopes in teen magazines, hoping to get some insight into your future? There is zero truth in those forms of prophesy, and besides, fortune telling is an activity the enemy uses to pull your faith away from Me. Place your trust in My direction, not in fantasy. I know your heart's desires, and My plans for your life are wonderful and complete. Don't worry about the process of getting there. Just concentrate on today's issues.

Now What? *Pray:* "Lord, it's tempting to want a glimpse of the future, but I know that none of us could handle that kind of insight. You know best and are careful only to reveal the steps of your plan that I am ready to receive. I place my future in your hands, Lord. I will follow your lead, not race ahead of you and hope you can catch up. Teach me to focus on each day and to trust you with what lies ahead."

I love you anyway . . .

"For by grace you have been saved through faith; and that not of yourselves, it is the gift of God; not as a result of works, so that no one may boast." - **Ephesians 2:8-9**

There's no need to spiff yourself up or put on a mask for Me. I can see straight through to the very heart of you, the *real* you. I know about your flaws and the problems you wrestle each day. I see every tear you cry, and I know which sins you struggle with the most. And I love you, mistakes and all. My grace is not something you earn by being "good enough." It's a gift I offer because you are My wonderful creation.

Now What? *Pray:* "O Lord, how wonderful is your love for me! I can hide my feelings and thoughts from everyone but you, and yet, you still love me, as imperfect as I am. I don't have to explain myself to you. I don't have to fill you in on painful details. Thank you, Jesus, for your reassurance and endless mercy."

by Lisa Cheater

In good times and bad . . .

"As Pharaoh approached, the Israelites looked up, and there were the Egyptians, marching after them. They were terrified and cried out to the LORD." - **Exodus 14:10 (NIV)**

Why do you wait to call upon Me until you are in the middle of a horrible crisis? Some of the problems you face could have been avoided in the first place if you had been talking to Me every day. Even if everything is going well, make talking with Me a daily habit you can't live without!

Now What? *Pray:* "Lord, when I don't talk with you each day I feel disconnected and emotionally weak, like a cell phone that needs charging. You are my lifeline, my strength, my hope, my path, my direction, and my comfort! Bless my time with you so much that I cannot wait to talk with you every day."

119

Faith is My gift to you . . .

"I do believe; help my unbelief." - **Mark 9:24**

Doubting doesn't mean you are no longer a Christian. I gave you a mind to think and reason and question, so faith isn't even possible without My help. Did you know that you can ask for Me to increase your faith if you're a constant doubter? When you feel uncertain and unsure about life, pray for strength and faith to feel confident in My power.

Now What? *Pray:* "Lord, my heart knows you are able to do anything, but sometimes my head prevents me from completely believing. There are times when my life seems so messed up that I have trouble seeing how you could straighten it up again. When I can't come up with answers, give me faith in your power, Jesus. Calm my fears and give me courage to rely on your Word and to ask for help instead of trying to solve problems all on my own."

by Lisa Cheater

One way . . .

"I am the way, and the truth, and the life; no one comes to the Father but through Me." - **John 14:6**

People spend their whole lives looking for "spiritual peace" when all they have to do is look at Me. Some argue that one way to Heaven, through Me, is too narrow-minded and not fair to other cultures, but I came for ALL cultures and ALL people! It doesn't get any broader than that! Resist the temptation to consider other religions. There's no need to look further for another truth. I *am* the Truth.

Now What? *Pray:* "Lord, so many things in this life are uncertain, and yet you remain constant and unchanging. I know I can always count on you to direct me in the right way, the way that is best for my life. Thank you for being my strong foundation and for the assurance of eternal life in Heaven."

121

Don't play favorites . . .

"My brethren, do not hold your faith in our glorious Lord Jesus Christ with an attitude of personal favoritism." - **James 2:1**

Do you show favoritism toward certain people? Are you more comfortable sitting next to someone who is popular, who dresses well or looks cute rather than someone dressed shabby or seems timid? What about someone of a different race? Choosing people based on how they look or what they have is discrimination and goes against all I teach. Show your love for Me by loving all people, regardless of their appearance or wealth.

Now What? *Pray:* "Father, help me remember that you created all people groups, and you love everyone equally as your children. Forgive me for harboring prejudice against anyone or for dismissing people who are different from me. Help me see all individuals through your eyes, and give me the opportunity to share your love with those who are in need. May I be careful to avoid discrimination and to include others as I walk through this day."

by Lisa Cheater

My love is bigger than your problems ...

"The LORD'S loving kindnesses indeed never cease, for His compassions never fail. They are new every morning; Great is Your faithfulness." - **Lamentations 3:22-23**

You get so ahead of yourself, worrying about tomorrow, next week, next month. Every day brings new challenges, yes, but it also brings new joys. Instead of dwelling on everything that's gone wrong, zero in on what is blessed about this day. Think of the many good things that I have given you, big and small, and worry will evaporate!

Now What? *Pray:* "Jesus, I often overlook the small yet amazing blessings you provide me each day. Just rising from sleep this morning is a wonderful gift! I have so many things weighing on my mind, but today, instead of being preoccupied with problems, let me see the good things about this day such as: ___(name 3 blessings)___. Thank you for these gifts, Lord!"

No one size . . .

"Now there are varieties of gifts, but the same Spirit. And there are varieties of ministries, and the same Lord." - **1 Corinthians 12:4-5**

What if Disney's Magic Kingdom only had ride workers? There'd be no food vendors, no ticket sellers, no clean bathrooms, no shuttle and monorail drivers. The place would collapse! I have created you to accomplish very specific tasks. You have skills and gifts that are unique and important. Don't waste your time wishing you had someone else's gift! They're all vital to the building up of My kingdom! Think about your talent, be grateful, and use it!

Now What? *Pray:* "Jesus, I am often confronted with feelings of inadequacy. I see the cool things my friends can do, and I long to be like them. But I realize now that you have designed me with a specific purpose and with specific gifts and talents. I know you have made me good at ____(name a skill)____. Help me fine-tune that ability and use it in ways that bring you glory."

by Lisa Cheater

Train those thoughts . . .

"...taking every thought captive to the obedience of Christ." - **2 Corinthians 10:5**

You know actions begin as an idea, so how can you make a thought "obedient" to Me? As soon as a tempting or wrong thought pops into your head, immediately pray, "Jesus, please remove My interest in this." Shift your mind from that line of evil thinking, and stop what you're doing if you have to. Move away from the computer, turn off the TV, put away your phone, or go talk to a Christian friend. Don't give the enemy a chance to trip you by entering your thoughts.

Now What? *Pray:* "Lord, thank you for creating prayer as a way for me to escape negative and destructive thoughts! Give me the ability to recognize when the enemy is invading my life through the way I think about myself and others. Grant me the strength to counter lies with your Truths: I AM made holy by your death and resurrection. I AM perfectly beautiful in your sight. I AM learning every day to become more like you. I AM totally loved and forgiven!"

Heads up . . .

"I who speak to you am He." - **John 4:26**

Every human is born with a need to feel and give love, to enjoy contentment, and to live a life full of meaning and worth. Some people try all kinds of things to fill these needs in their lives: drugs, alcohol, sexual attention, even food. But when you move away from Me, your life becomes chaotic and restless. You may even wonder why I'm not answering your prayers or if I've abandoned you. In those times, remember that I never left. Don't look for Me in a change of situation. Just be still, study my Word, and trust Me in all circumstances.

Now What? *Pray:* "Jesus, you are the answer to every question I have. You are the water that fills my empty soul. Teach me to seek you in all things, in all circumstances, no matter how big or small. May prayer become a habit I can't live without, and may the promises in scripture become the songs of my heart. Keep me close to you, Lord, as I mature and encounter whatever the future holds for me."

by Lisa Cheater

Refuse the risk ...

"Do not be deceived: 'Bad company corrupts good morals.'" -
1 Corinthians 15:33

At times, your parents may try to steer you away from certain individuals or activities because they say they're a bad influence on you. Listen to them! I give you direction in human form through your parents, church leaders, authorities, and teachers. No matter how strong a Christian you may be, socializing and cavorting with non-Believers can lead you astray. Pray for those people, invite them to church, but don't be pulled into their social circles.

Now What? *Pray:* "Jesus, people are sometimes hard to figure out because they aren't always who they seem to be at first. I desire friendships that please you, that strengthen me as a Believer, and that encourage others. Teach me to recognize and be drawn to people who are strong in their faith, so that I will not falter in my Christian walk. Remove opportunities for me to fall into the wrong social circles and keep my attitude positive toward my parents and other leaders who love me and have been sent to guide me."

127

Second wind . . .

"To You, O LORD, I lift up my soul." - **Psalms 25:1**

When you feel beaten down by the world, life can seem as though you're running the last mile of a marathon. You want to keep going, but you're so tired and frustrated. Rather than giving in and throwing in the towel, kneel on it instead. If you can't think of the right words to describe your grief, just pray this verse to Me. I'll know what you mean and help you finish the race.

Now What? *Pray:* "To You, Lord Jesus, I lift up my soul. I give you everything happening in my life right now, my plans, my goals, and my choices. Lead me in all the ways I should go. I love you, Jesus, for you are my comforter and friend."

by Lisa Cheater

Obey your parents ...

"Honor your father and your mother, so that you may live long in the land the LORD your God is giving you." - **Exodus 20:12 (NIV)**

It's important to Me that you obey the godly direction of your parents, even if you feel they're being unfair and unreasonable. Respecting and following their leadership is not a request from me; it's a commandment, and I hold parents highly accountable for the life they live before their children. People who scoff at and deliberately disobey sound authority will eventually find themselves in serious trouble. I want to bless your life, to make it long and fruitful! Someday you'll be on your own, and accepting the control of those I have put over you for now is one way to secure those future blessings.

Now What? *Pray:* "Father God, I know in my heart when the direction I receive from my parents, teachers or leaders is from you because it is supported by scripture. The rules I break most often aren't merely household rules; they are commandments and teachings of the Bible. Forgive me for rebelling against your authority by arguing with my parents and failing to obey their direction. Today, help me respectfully accept their guidance."

129

I've seen it all ...

"About the ninth hour Jesus cried out with a loud voice, saying, 'Eli Eli, lama sabachthani?' that is, 'My God, My God, why have you forsaken Me?'" - **Matthew 27:46**

Every emotion you are capable of feeling, I have felt, too. When I was on the cross, in My very darkest moment, I felt like My Father had abandoned Me there, and I asked him why. Still, I knew His way was perfect and that His love would triumph. I'm not some unreachable god far removed from the worries of the world. I know exactly how it feels to be discouraged, betrayed, hated, loved, grieved, and injured, so take heart. A beautiful, joy-filled future awaits for those who place their trust in Me. Talk to Me, and I'll give you the strength you need to endure heartbreak.

Now What? *Pray:* "Jesus, you are wise and mighty, and I love you for coming into the world to identify with the challenges that face me every day. You understand completely. I can choose to let my disappointments and problems rob me of happiness, or I can choose to be positive in the middle of every crisis. I will start today by praising you no matter how sad or tired I am. Then give me wisdom as I read your Word, to learn from how you handled your emotions and setbacks."

by Lisa Cheater

Not in the words . . .

"Before they call I will answer; while they are still speaking I will hear."- **Isaiah 65:24 (NIV)**

I begin answering your prayers the *instant* you turn your thoughts to Me, not after you've finished praying a specific prayer. Praying the "correct" words is not what moves Me. Your attitude of surrender is what gets the ball rolling! Don't try to solve everything on your own. Release your pride and need to control, and call on the power of My name. I hear you and am already answering.

Now What? *Pray:* "Lord, sometimes I am so overwhelmed with grief that I can't formulate *any* words to pray, much less the right ones, and my heart can only cry out in tears of sadness. I am so glad you understand my needs and know exactly what is best for my life, even if the right answer is 'wait' or 'no.' When I feel like rolling into a ball and hiding in my room, give me strength to just turn my thoughts to you, knowing you are already to my rescue. Thank you, Jesus, for your infinite mercy."

Hold on tight . . .

"Many are the afflictions of the righteous, But the LORD delivers him out of them all." - **Psalms 34:19**

It's hard to believe this promise when you are in the middle of a nasty crisis. My ways are so contrary to how the world wants you to live. It'd be easier just to give in to sin and do whatever you want, but that choice leads to certain destruction. The path you have chosen with Me leads to love, peace, safety and assurance. When life becomes agonizing, and the hills are too steep to climb, I will carry you.

Now What? *Pray:* "Jesus, I am claiming this promise, that every trial, every struggle, will have an end. Reveal to my heart if I am the cause of any problems in my life: Am I being stubborn? Am I holding onto resentment and bitterness? Am I unwilling to forgive someone? Am I choosing to sin against your commands? I know these actions will only prolong my troubles, so today enable me to break free of any thing or behavior that displeases you."

by Lisa Cheater

Show yourself respect . . .

"Do you not know that you are a temple of God and that the Spirit of God dwells in you?" - **1 Corinthians 3:16**

You are a holy place! I live through each one who believes in Me as Savior, and that makes everything about you very important to me: where you go, what you hear, what you consume, what you say and do. I allow you to make choices for yourself, but I *want* you to choose Me. Make sure everything you do protects your physical body, mind, and reputation.

Now What? *Pray:* "Jesus, thank you for the wonderful gift of life. I know it's my job to take care of the body you've entrusted to me, and I ask you to help me take that responsibility seriously. I commit to you that I will make time for rest, eat healthy, keep myself sexually pure until marriage, and choose to enjoy movies and music that encourage a lifestyle pleasing to you."

Just one life . . .

"What man among you, if he has a hundred sheep and has lost one of them, does not leave the ninety-nine in the open pasture and go after the one which is lost until he finds it?" - **Luke 15:4**

Have you ever lost something so important to you that you couldn't think of anything else until you found it? I feel that way about every Believer who chooses to go astray. I never say, "Eh, he's just one life out of millions. I've got plenty of other sheep to lead." Every person is infinitely loved by Me, and I long for rebellious hearts to turn back to me. I will never give up on you and your potential to accomplish mighty things. No matter how much you may struggle in your Christian walk or how old you are, you will always be My precious child.

Now What? *Pray:* "Lord Jesus, thank you for loving me. Remind me of this scripture, that I am your coveted sheep, whenever I feel inadequate and beat down. I matter to you, even if I don't always feel like it, even if people around me don't say it enough. You say it through your scripture, through the understanding I receive from the Holy Spirit when I read the Bible and observe every creation in nature. I am yours. Always."

by Lisa Cheater

Bring it on!

"The LORD also will be a stronghold for the oppressed, A stronghold in times of trouble;" - **Psalms 9:9**

Virtually every person has the same reaction to trouble: get out of it quickly! Just as the basement or interior room of your house is the safest place to hunker down during a tornado, I am your stronghold when life pummels you like a giant hurricane. You don't have to be a victim of your circumstances, no matter how bleak! With My help, you have the ability to weather any difficulty. Choose to bring your troubles to Me instead of despairing in the storm. I will protect you.

Now What? *Pray:* "Jesus, you are my safe place! Thank you for never leaving, never moving, never locking me out. Help me see that I am able to experience your protection in hard times whenever I focus my attention on you and your Word instead of my problems, and trust you with the outcomes, *without* worrying or complaining. Teach me to lean on you in all situations."

A pretty face . . .

"Do not let your heart turn aside to her ways, do not stray into her paths." - **Proverbs 7:25**

Satan does NOT have a forked tail and horns like you see in movies. In fact, he is beautiful, enticing, cunning, tasty, glittery—all the things you find appealing. That's what makes him so dangerous. It'd be easy to run from a flaming red devil, but very hard to turn from an alluring non-Christian, a hilarious dirty movie, alcohol, or a sexy picture on the internet. If you feel being drawn into something that you would not want Me to see, get away from there as fast as you can.

Now What? *Pray:* "Jesus, I know temptation is something we all struggle with, but I confess that I specifically wrestle against the temptation of ____(name it)____. Lord, I want to break free from the stronghold this sin has around me. Please strengthen my faith in your Word and your promises so I can say 'no' the next time I am confronted by the overwhelming lure of sin. Protect me form places and situations that might lead me astray."

by Lisa Cheater

It WILL get better . . .

"Weeping may last for the night, but a shout of joy comes in the morning." - **Psalms 30:5**

Don't try to stuff all your emotions inside. When you are hurting and disappointed, it's perfectly okay to cry and release the anxiety that's built up in your heart. There's no need to hurt yourself by wallowing in your pain or physically damaging your body, My temple! You may be sad or despairing now, but tomorrow brings new possibilities and a chance to for you to look to Me and say, "Okay. Let's start over."

Now What? *Pray:* "Jesus, thank you for being the Lord of second chances (and third, and fourth...). When I'm at my lowest, I will remember this scripture, that "joy comes in the morning" if I place my trust in you. But in those moments before the morning, Lord, let me feel your close presence and assurance that my time of sadness will, indeed, pass."

Want vs. need . . .

"He gives rain on the earth and sends water on the fields..." - **Job 5:10**

Do you really know the difference between a want and a need? You may want the top-of-the-line phone or an Xbox®, but do you *need* them? Need is something you cannot live without: food, shelter, care. Avoid envying celebrities and people around you who spend tons of cash on things they don't need. If I granted you everything you wanted, you could easily become greedy and *still* not feel satisfied. I promise to take care of your needs as you walk with Me. The rest is all gravy!

Now What? *Pray:* "Father, you provide everything I need, from a place to live to food and clothing. I know some of the things I want are definitely not needs; there are just so many cool things out there! Show me when my wants are becoming doorways for Satan to bring jealousy, discontent, anger, and sin into my heart. Thank you for all the things you have given me. You are gracious, Lord!"

by Lisa Cheater

Power up . . .

"...In repentance and rest you will be saved, in quietness and trust is your strength." - **Isaiah 30:15**

These words do not describe the typical teen who is often anxious, rambunctious, noisy, scattered, and busy. Spending time with Me is usually last on your list, but at this rapid pace, you'll burn out just like some old MP3 player. This verse paints a great picture of how to recharge your spiritual batteries. Stop for a moment. Shut out the craziness of the world, crack open that Bible, and listen to My voice through the scriptures as though each word is a personal message. That's how you renew your courage to make it through each day.

Now What? *Pray:* "Lord, my world seems to get noisier every day. Technology is partly to blame, but so am I. I don't make enough time to talk to you and listen. I argue that I can't hear your voice, but that's not true. Your voice is all around me, through words of scripture and through the Christian direction of my parents, ministers, and leaders. Encourage me to shut down all the sounds in my life each day so I can connect to you, *my* power source."

Mighty humble . . .

"Humble yourselves in the presence of the Lord, and He will exalt you." - **James 4:10**

Humbleness is often the opposite of how the world defines "strong". You try so hard to make others believe you are capable, smart, and right, you fail to see that humility is what's important to Me. Not *humiliation* (which is what happens when you spill spaghetti down your shirt at lunch), but *humbleness*, the attitude that you are not God, I am, and that I am in control of all things, not you. Those who relinquish control to Me will be blessed!

Now What? *Pray:* "Lord, give me an attitude of humbleness and trust. Break any rebellious spirit within me that prevents you from leading and blessing me. I cannot compete with your greatness and wisdom, Lord, for you are a Holy God who knows, *always*, what is best for me. I am not capable of making things happen or changing other people. Thank you for strengthening me through my willingness to submit to your authority."

by Lisa Cheater

140

Sin's dead end . . .

"For the wages of sin is death, but the free gift of God is eternal life in Christ Jesus our Lord." - **Romans 6:23**

Every sin, left unchecked, winds up at the same place - death. Think about it. Even a tiny sin can lead to a pattern of destructive behavior that can make you physically ill or take you into places that are life threatening. Don't make excuses for your small indiscretions. You know when you've done wrong. Confess it to Me, and have your heart wiped clean so you won't be lured down evil's slippery slope.

Now What? *Pray:* "God, reveal to me if there are any destructive patterns of behavior in my life. Am I consistently "one-upping" from one sin to the next, blind to the fact that they are getting bigger and more serious each time? Teach me to remember that I am not a slave to sin. Every morning I have the ability to choose your path of life and peace."

141

Blessed strength . . .

"Be strong and courageous. Do not be afraid or terrified because of them, for the LORD your God goes with you; he will never leave you nor forsake you. - **Deuteronomy 31:6 (NIV)**

Life Situquation #3: You + Faith in Me = Power to Overcome Anything

Now What? *Pray:* "God, I am in awe of your power. I do not have to be afraid of anything or anyone because you go before me. Wherever I travel, whenever I have a performance or a tough confrontation, you are already there, setting up protective safeguards and providing me with the words I should say. Thank you, Father, for your all-seeing guidance."

by Lisa Cheater

The job of all believers . . .

"...you will receive power when the Holy Spirit has come upon you; and you shall be My witnesses both in Jerusalem, and in all Judea and Samaria, and even to the remotest part of the earth." - **Acts 1:8**

Every Christian is expected to tell others about Me, often with words, but always by how they live their lives. Your "Jerusalem" is the place where you are every day - your neighborhood, your family, and your friends at school. Be a witness before them first, then try participating in a short term mission trip to a nearby community or state (your "Judea and Samaria"), or maybe a new country (the "remotest parts"). Don't be intimidated. I'll guide your steps and words.

Now What? *Pray:* "Lord, forgive me for not sharing hope with those you have placed in my path. Who are the people you want me to pray for? Who needs you in their life? One person you bring to my mind is: _____ (name)_____. Help me set my attitude right each day so that my life may be a positive witness before this person and others, and should the opportunity arise, give me boldness to tell them how you have blessed my life."

143

Good from bad ...

"And we know that God causes all things to work together for good to those who love God, to those who are called according to His purpose."- **Romans 8:28**

Life doesn't always make sense. Situations may seem unfair or impossible, but I am always in control of what happens to you, even if it doesn't seem so. I am busy in the background, orchestrating things to bless you down the road. I can turn any situation around and use it for the glory of My Father. Even when bad things happen, trust Me to create something positive out of the negative.

Now What? *Pray:* "Lord Jesus, I do not understand your ways or how you work all things together for my good, but I will trust you. Help me see that by closing doors, you are able to direct my path. Through hard times, you are able to strengthen my faith. In disappointments, you are able to draw me closer. Lord, I thank you for every challenge I face, for you will bring something good from each one."

Be still!

"Be still, and know that I am God." - **Psalms 46:10 (NIV)**

Have you ever tried to capture a puppy that's intent on playing? It's almost impossible. The more you try to catch it, the faster and further he runs. You are often like that, running from My Word, from My persistent whispers. I long to tell you things, direct your future and help you with your struggles, but you just keep running and moving. Settle down and talk with Me. I am here, ready to give good news of encouragement if you'll listen.

Now What? *Pray:* "Jesus, I get so wrapped up in my daily routine and activities that I often miss your subtle messages of love: the glorious sunrise, the rain that protects us from drought, the very food I eat. I take so many things for granted! When I sit down to dinner tonight, remind me to *really* thank you for your blessings. Even for that moment, let me be still and remember that you are watching over me."

145

Who's the richest?

*"For where jealousy and selfish ambition exist, there is disorder and every evil thing." - **James 3:16***

Some celebrities seem to have it all, don't they? Money, clothes, cars, beauty, fabulous trips... But if you had My perspective, you'd see the full story. You'd see their sleeplessness, pride, jealousy, fear, sadness, and emptiness. Selfishness is one of the enemy's favorite tools. It drives people to want more, but more is never enough. Don't be fooled by the glitz you see on television and in magazines. You already have access to the ultimate contentment that is more valuable than money: Me.

Now What? *Pray:* "Lord, as I am getting older and beginning to think about college, work, and my future, teach me to understand the difference between goals and selfish ambition. I want to use the specific talents and skills you've given me to bring glory to you and expand your kingdom. If my goals don't align with that objective, give me the strength to let them go and reset my priorities."

by Lisa Cheater

146

Spotlight is on ...

"If we confess our sins, He is faithful and righteous to forgive us our sins and to cleanse us from all unrighteousness." - **1 John 1:9**

When you were little, you occasionally thought you could get out of trouble by denying fault. "I dunno...not me!" was your standard answer to "Who did this?" That doesn't work so great anymore, does it? Parents usually know the answer to those kinds of questions. I *always* know the answer. I see everything you do, but your confession, your admission of guilt by telling the truth, is needed for forgiveness. Only until you confess with your mouth and heart, can I hear your prayers. That's how Truth sets you free.

Now What? *Pray:* "Lord, I know I cannot experience your forgiveness unless I first admit where I am wrong. My sin is the only thing that stands between us, so today, I confess to you this area where I know I have fallen short of your expectations: _____(name it)_____. Jesus, forgive me for this sin, cleanse my heart of guilt and self-doubt, and protect me from repeating this mistake. Thank you for your incredible gift of mercy. I love you, Jesus."

147

If you had your way . . .

"The LORD is slow to anger and great in power, and the LORD will by no means leave the guilty unpunished." - **Nahum 1:3**

I am very patient, but I will not allow those who consistently dishonor My Father through sin to go on forever without judgment, especially those who call themselves Christians. Hard consequences follow rebellion, and I often provide many opportunities for My children to make the right choice before I step back and allow those consequences to catch up with them. Stay on the path that follows Me so I can bless your life with contentment.

> Now What? *Pray:* "God, you alone are fair and righteous! This scripture is a strong reminder for me to consciously avoid life's many sinful temptations, but it also encourages me to know that you are aware of all the evil in the world, and in your own time, you *will* bring about justice. Thank you for never giving up on me!"

by Lisa Cheater

Shine on!

"I am the LORD, I have called you in righteousness, I will also hold you by the hand and watch over you, and I will appoint you as a covenant to the people, as a light to the nations..." - **Isaiah 42:6**

Do you not see how much I love you? Nothing could ever make Me stop adoring you. My plans for you are tremendous, and no one else is able to do the things I know you are capable of doing now and in the future. Everything good you do is like a billboard ad for hope; the people around you are desperate to know that love still exists in the world. Show them! For you are My shining star, My precious light in the darkness.

Now What? *Pray:* "Jesus, I am faced daily with situations that are scary and overwhelming, and I do not have the ability to confront and overcome them on my own. I often do not feel worthy to be called your ambassador or even a "good example" of Christianity. Lord, let me feel your presence right now, with your arms around me and your strength within me. Help me change my ways to align with yours so that others may see you in me. Though I don't deserve it, thank you for choosing me, Lord."

149

Different love ...

"The one who does not love does not know God, for God is love." -
1 John 4:8

There is more than one kind of love. The dizzy, "I'm in sooooo in love with___" is referred to as *Eros* love. *Philia* love describes the love you have for a best friend. Both of these love types usually depend on a situation or positive relationship, but *Agape* is the love I have for you, and it's the love I want you show to others, even people you don't know. It rises above all other loves because it's boundless and not tied to perfection or a feeling.

> Now What? *Pray:* "Father, grant me wisdom to discern different types of love, to know when someone's claim is genuine or just words. Do my closest friends demonstrate love through gentleness, patience, peace and joy? Do I back up my claims of love with faithfulness, self-control and kindness? Thank you, God, for your never-ending *agape* love that is not contingent upon how perfect I am."

by Lisa Cheater

Where the real blame lies . . .

"Be self-controlled and alert. Your enemy the devil prowls around like a roaring lion looking for someone to devour." - **1 Peter 5:8 (NIV)**

Don't bother directing your anger toward individuals who have wronged you. Your ultimate battle is with Satan, whose goal is for you to stumble, doubt God's power, question your Salvation, and destroy your relationships, especially with family members. The enemy is the ringmaster behind every evil word and hurtful deed. Pray for God, My Father, to bind evil and give you the wisdom to avoid Satan's tricks.

> Now What? *Pray:* "Lord, I should not be surprised when I feel as though I am facing evil at every turn; I am! But you are mightier than any evil! Protect me from Satan's attacks upon my faith and my relationships with others, especially other Christians. Prevent me from directing my anger towards other people. Post your army of angels around me today, and focus my thoughts on your promises in scripture."

Holding grudges . . .

"If You, LORD, should mark iniquities, O Lord, who could stand?" -
Psalms 130:3

I do not remember your past forgiven sins, and any guilt you feel over past mistakes is coming from the enemy, not Me. Even still, you are often quick to rehash every little thing that's ever been done against you! If you need to repair a relationship, go do it, then move on. I don't hold grudges and neither should you.

> Now What? *Pray:* "Jesus, I confess I am holding a grudge against: _____(name person)_____. My unforgiveness has felt like a thorn in my hand for long enough. Even if this person never apologizes to me, I want to let go of my bitterness toward him/her right now. We are all imperfect, and I am grateful for the love and forgiveness you offer me. Help me extend that kind of mercy to others."

by Lisa Cheater

152

You are mighty . . .

"Therefore put on the full armor of God, so that when the day of evil comes, you may be able to stand your ground, and after you have done everything, to stand." - **Ephesians 6:13 (NIV)**

Evil is everywhere, but remember, I have given you many weapons to defend yourself against Darkness! What is the "Armor of God"? Truth and Righteousness protect your heart from sadness. The Gospel is like a pair of shoes that support you wherever you go. Faith in My power is your shield, and Salvation is like a helmet that guards your mind against destructive thoughts and despair. Most of all, remember that My Word, the Bible, is a sharp sword against all evil. With these tools, you can defeat any scheme of Satan!

Now What? *Pray:* "Father, I thank you for all the tools you have made available to protect me from evil! Yes, it's a crazy, flipped-upside-down, often godless, world, but with the weapons I received at the moment of my salvation, I do not have to be afraid or despair. You are my mighty general and leader in every one of life's battles. Thank you, Lord, for your incredible strength and power!"

153

Pray before you Google . . .

"Come to Me, all who are weary and heavy-laden, and I will give you rest." - **Matthew 11:28**

The Internet is an amazing tool. You can access all kinds of information and instructions for doing just about anything, but it doesn't always provide peace of mind. Don't let some Web chat room or social media outlet be your first choice for solving a difficult problem. Come to Me and pray. No matter what burden you carry right now, the best answers are in the Bible, not Wikipedia. Seek the unshakable truth that only comes from My Eternalnet!

Now What? *Pray:* "Jesus, you always have the right answers, the best answers, but sometimes I don't turn to you first because *I* may have to change the way I look at my situation. Lord, you never promised me a worry-free life, only that you would always be here to comfort and guide. So, as I walk though this day, I will seek you first when I encounter a problem or disappointment."

by Lisa Cheater

154

Either way . . .

"If it be so, our God whom we serve is able to deliver us from the furnace of blazing fire; and He will deliver us out of your hand, O king."- **Daniel 3:17**

The hardest part about asking Me for something is realizing I may choose not to answer the way you want. Be okay with that, because however I choose to answer your prayers will be what's best for you, even if you disagree. My love for you is huge, and because I see far into your future, I know exactly what to give you for today. I rejoice when you give total control to Me because it shows your faith in My sovereignty.

Now What? *Pray:* "Father, I struggle most with the first four words of this verse, *'If it be so,'* because it requires me to give my will over to you. Help me understand that in giving you control, my prayers are answered! The outcome will always be perfect according to your will and best for me. Teach me to always begin my requests with these four words, to immediately hand over control of every situation to you and to be content with your answers."

155

Tough love ...

"But Jesus was saying, 'Father, forgive them; for they do not know what they are doing.' And they cast lots, dividing up His garments among themselves." - **Luke 23:34**

Even in My darkest hour I believed in the plan of My Father. I knew He would create something glorious out of My suffering, and still, I forgave those who tortured and murdered Me without reason. Don't you think you can forgive someone who has treated you poorly?

Now What? *Pray:* "Jesus, the depth of your love and forgiveness is boundless! I offer up to you this person: ____(name them)____, someone I, frankly, do not like because of how they treat me and others. Oh, how they need you! Instead of hating them, I am asking you to intervene in his /her life, to reach into their soul and soften a very hard heart. I am excited to see how you will work in this person, Lord!"

by Lisa Cheater

The road to Heaven . . .

"And someone came to Him and said, 'Teacher, what good thing shall I do that I may obtain eternal life?'" - **Matthew 19:16**

So many people think Heaven is a place for those whose good deeds outweigh the bad. That idea leads to a life filled with guilt and constant measurement, not joy and assurance! No one is perfect or good enough to earn a spot in Heaven. Only by believing that I came to die for you and choosing to spend your life following My teachings will you be guaranteed a place in paradise.

Now What? *Pray:* "Lord, if a future in Heaven was dependent upon how good I am, I'd never make it in—none of us would! Forgive me for judging myself and other people against a measuring stick I made up. Belief in your life, death, burial and resurrection is all I need. Thank you for making a way for cranky, unholy people to have a relationship with a Holy God."

The wise listen . . .

"Through [prideful disrespect] comes nothing but strife, but wisdom is with those who receive counsel." - **Proverbs 13:10**

It's sometimes hard for you to ask for help or admit you're wrong. Doing so makes you feel like you've lost some argument, like a helpless child. But the opposite is true. Your pride and determination to be right keep you from enjoying a close relationship with Me, and arguing only makes you anxious and irritable. Asking for help and fessing up when you're wrong are signs of intelligence and maturity, proof of my Spirit in you.

Now What? *Pray:* "Lord, why do I fight against authority and help? You have placed specific people in my life at school, at home, at church, and in my community to serve as your speakers. They're like ear buds plugged into a divine iPod! Remove my habit of feeling threatened and stupid when I am offered counsel. Instead, remind me to immediately thank you for those words of wisdom that serve to guide and keep me on the right path."

by Lisa Cheater

Bully ≠ Strong . . .

"Blessed are the gentle, for they shall inherit the earth." - **Matthew 5:5**

Action movies often portray the hero as tough and strong, the guy who finally whoops-up on the evil villain. The early Jews believed their Messiah would be like that. They were disappointed in Me, because they wanted a vicious warrior, and My strength came from wisdom and gentleness, not by a sword. I didn't ridicule and scream at the sinners I met. I loved them and spoke to them out of deep concern. Bullies are not strong. They are weak and full of self-doubt. They hurt others to make themselves look tough. Model your behavior after Me, and let Me be your hero.

Now What? *Pray:* "Jesus, I am surrounded by people who believe that winners are the ones who yell the loudest, push the hardest, rule the fiercest, *and* have the most friends on Facebook®. I want to be a winner in your eyes, even if that ideal is way different than what the world dictates. Help me be strong by being in control at all times, leading with encouragement and shouting with of words of praise to you!"

Don't be fooled . . .

"On whom are you depending, that you rebel against me?" - **Isaiah 36:5b (NIV)**

Throughout history, evil people have tried to mislead the godly by promising all kinds of things: fame and fortune, power and glory. If you are My follower you will recognize My voice, that inner discomfort that tells you when something's not right. If you are confused by someone's words, ask yourself, "Is this Jesus speaking to me? Is this something He would say?" If you have a doubt, leave it out. Don't ever be afraid to walk away from a deceiver.

Now What? *Pray:* "Jesus, although I am pushed and pulled from so many different directions, I am learning that there are really only two forces at work in my life: yours and the enemy's. Through my thoughts and behavior, I choose to side with one or the other. Sometimes the wrong choice is easy to spot, but at other times, it's confusing and not so straightforward. Especially in those times, Lord, show me the way I should go. Let me hear your voice above all others. Always."

by Lisa Cheater

It's not all about you …

"Do not merely look out for your own personal interests, but also for the interests of others. Have this attitude in yourselves which was also in Christ Jesus…" - **Philippians 2:4-5**

At your age, it's so tempting to see only yourself in the center of life's universe. You wonder why other people make things so difficult by not seeing things your way. Realize that living *for* Me means living *like* Me, and that requires selflessness. As you go through today, look for opportunities to help another person. Carry the books of someone on crutches, help your mom do the dishes, sit and talk with an elderly neighbor for a moment. I will bless you for sacrificing your time to the help of others!

Now What? *Pray:* "Lord Jesus, it's so easy to get wrapped up in my day-to-day schedule and activities that I miss the needs of other people. I lose sight that every day I am to spend building up myself and others for your Kingdom. How can I show how much I love you by ministering to someone else today? Grant me the opportunity and astute eyes to clearly recognize someone in need."

161

Forgiveness doesn't relieve consequences...

"Then when Judas, who had betrayed Him, saw that He had been condemned, he felt remorse and returned the thirty pieces of silver to the chief priests and elders..." - **Matthew 27:3**

Even after Judas realized he'd made a fatal mistake of turning Me over to the Romans, he couldn't escape the inevitable consequences coming his way. He lost his place in My group of followers, and, eventually, his life. I am faithful to forgive your sins when you confess them, but that doesn't mean you automatically get out of trouble. Sin often carries a heavy price. Is it worth it?

Now What? *Pray:* "No, Jesus, no sin, pleasure, or moments of fleeting popularity is worth the penalty. I want my life to make you smile! I want to experience a blessed life that comes from pleasing you and following your will. Open my eyes to my own behavior. Give me courage to acknowledge my sins and accept the consequences of my actions. Forgive me for my selfishness, and restore my relationship with you where no secrets exist."

by Lisa Cheater

162

Hold your tongue . . .

"The tongue also is a fire, a world of evil among the parts of the body. It corrupts the whole person, sets the whole course of his life on fire, and is itself set on fire by hell." - **James 3:6 (NIV)**

Entire wars have been started over harsh words. For such a small body part, the tongue can do tremendous harm. It's like a hand grenade sent straight from the enemy. Unleashed, the tongue can ruin relationships, wound feelings, and obliterate trust. Be very careful before you let your words slip out uncontrolled. Think first about how you should respond rather than react. It's better to let Me handle the issue than to make things worse by adding fuel to an argument.

Now What? *Pray:* "Jesus, thank you for this reminder. Cursing and hate-filled words fly around me all day, so much so that I have almost become immune to their effects—unless they're targeted at me. Do I do that to others? Are my words helpful in building up people or do they tear people down? Filter my speech, Lord. Clear my thoughts of malice and hate. Teach me to think before I speak, and may my words reflect how much I love you."

Ok to squeeze the fruit . . .

"You will know them by their fruits. Grapes are not gathered from thorn bushes nor figs from thistles, are they?" - **Matthew 7:16**

Only I can see inside a person's heart, but My true followers will exhibit fruits of the sprit that are indeed visible: gentleness, patience, kindness, longsuffering, faith, love, joy, goodness, and self-control. When considering a date or close friendship, look for evidence of these characteristics, especially if someone claims to be a Christian. But avoid thinking you are better than others in judgment. Remember, these are measures of your spiritual attitude as well.

Now What? *Pray:* "First, Lord, as I look at this list of nine spiritual fruits, I know I struggle most with _____ (name it)_____. Help me develop that characteristic through opportunities to practice it. Then steer me away from destructive relationships and individuals. Lead me to strong Christian friends who boldly live out their faith so that I may be encouraged in my walk."

by Lisa Cheater

164

Against the grain . . .

"I am the LORD your God. You must not do as they do in Egypt, where you used to live, and you must not do as they do in the land of Canaan, where I am bringing you. Do not follow their practices." - **Leviticus 18:2-3 (NIV)**

Peer pressure is a real and difficult experience for every teenager. At an age where fitting in seems most important, you are asked by Me to go against the flow and do what's right rather than what's popular. You may lose "friends" in the process. But understand that only My opinion of you matters, and don't allow pals or classmates to corrupt your solid character. People who badmouth or berate you for doing what's right are definitely *not* friends.

Now What? *Pray:* "Lord, I offer my slate of friends up to you, and if there is one who encourages me to compromise my faith and do things I know are wrong, I ask you to dissolve that relationship. Reach into their heart and change them, for I know that I am not capable of changing anyone except myself. Thank you, Jesus, for providing scripture and your model to follow so I don't have to wonder what's right and wrong."

Listen to your dad...

"A wise son accepts his father's discipline, but a scoffer does not listen to rebuke." - **Proverbs 13:1**

There is nothing better than a godly mom and dad. I have placed you in the care of your parents, and I hold them responsible for you, which includes your discipline. You demonstrate your love for Me by obeying your parents' rules and respecting their advice. They correct you because they love you and want you to stay away from paths of destruction. Even if you disagree with them, be wise. Listen.

Now What? *Pray:* "Jesus, because I love you, because I know you love me, I will honor and obey my parents and leaders. I will not complain, I will not whine. This is my covenant with you. Thank you, Lord, for those you have charged with my care."

by Lisa Cheater

Keep pure . . .

"Do not desire her beauty in your heart, nor let her capture you with her eyelids." - **Proverbs 6:25**

Human beings are My most honored and cherished creation, and there's nothing more wonderful than gazing moony-eyed at a cute guy or girl. I designed you to love, to worship Me, and to be loved, but be wary of lust. Lust is a desire to physically want someone to whom you are not married. The Bible is clear that lust is sin and very often leads to heartache. Don't let yourself be seduced. Wait for sex with the person I have chosen for you.

Now What? *Pray:* "Lord, thank you for creating the gifts of love and sex within marriage. Surround me with your angels of light and protect me from temptation and lust so that I can remain pure until I meet my future spouse. It's not too early for me to ask you to bless and guard that person you've chosen for me. May they also be committed to purity until we meet and are joined in your sight."

Ripe for blessing . . .

"Blessed are those who hunger and thirst for righteousness, for they shall be satisfied." - **Matthew 5:6**

Your world is full of people who are just itching to start a fight and create havoc. They seem to thrive on disorder and arguments because they see it as a way to get attention and make themselves appear strong. My followers, on the other hand, always want goodness to prevail. They long for justice in all circumstances and rejoice in triumph over sin. *That* is the measure of true strength. Choose the path of goodness so I can bless your life with joy.

Now What? *Pray:* "Lord, thank you for your guidance and justice. I know the only way I will be able to recognize justice or injustice, true goodness or temptation, is to be immersed in the Bible. Compel me to carve out time in every day to read and study scripture. Embed your words into my heart and mind so I can stand confident against sin."

by Lisa Cheater

Yes, you HAVE to clean your room . . .

"...the Jews do not eat unless they carefully wash their hands, thus observing the traditions of the elders; and when they come from the market place, they do not eat unless they cleanse themselves..." - **Mark 7:3-4**

Early Jewish law required people wash up before dinner, just like you. They were required to clean all the pots and dishes, too. Cleanliness is just as important today. Here's why: cleaning your room (which your parents own) shows appreciation for what they have provided for you. Washing up before a meal also shows respect for their rules and keeps you healthy. If cleaning up seems like mindless chore and a big waste of time, maybe you need to slow down and reprioritize.

Now What? *Pray:* "God, help me see cleaning with new eyes. Let me regard it not as a chore, but as a way of pleasing you directly. By helping maintain my space, I can show my gratitude to you (and my parents) for all my stuff and my home. Thank you, for the things and guardians you have given me."

169

I answer every prayer . . .

"The LORD hears when I call to Him." - **Psalms 4:3**

Your prayers are like a lifeline to Me. I hear and answer every one. No sound makes Me happier than that of your voice calling on My name, but don't be discouraged if it feels like I've taken a vacation or haven't given you the answer you desire. Trust Me in times of waiting. I am working on parts of your future you have yet to see and in the lives of people you have yet to meet. Be patient. I have heard you.

Now What? *Pray:* "Father, sometimes it does seem like you have put me on call waiting. I can't hear your voice. I don't know your plan. Lord, in those times when I feel like I'm treading water alone in the middle of the ocean, give me a supernatural peace. Restore my hope through some small encouragement: a kind word, a meaningful scripture, or a glorious sunset. I know you hear me. Help me to be patient while I wait for your answer."

by Lisa Cheater

All of you . . .

"Now those who belong to Christ Jesus have crucified the flesh with its passions and desires." - **Galatians 5:24**

Every Christian before you wrestled with sin, even great men and women of the Bible like Paul, Abraham, Sarah, and David. Becoming My follower doesn't eliminate your ability to *choose* the right behavior; it guides your decisions. If you know what is truly right, you'll be able to identify what isn't. Be patient with yourself, pray, study My word, and choose your closest friends carefully. Your old selfish desires will gradually melt away.

Now What? *Pray:* "Lord, thank you for the Bible and for its stories of real people, just like me, who weren't perfect either. I will not believe Satan's lies that I am not good enough. My Christian walk is a process where every day is another mile in that journey. I will not despair over setbacks and failures. I will learn from them, with your help, and move on."

Big picture perspective...

"Now I want you to know, brethren, that my circumstances have turned out for the greater progress of the gospel..." - **Philippians 1:12**

"God, what are you doing up there!!? Can't you see the mess I'm in? Why aren't you helping me?" I hear it all the time. Life throws you a serious curve ball, and you feel I've left you alone in the stadium. I promise you joy, contentment regardless of your circumstances, but not constant happiness. I see a much bigger picture of your life than you can possibly imagine. A challenge is often a good thing! Keep the faith and trust that I will use your difficult situation to strengthen your character.

Now What? *Pray:* "Jesus, it's so hard to say this, but I thank you for my challenges and difficulties. If I must endure a time of hardship in order to stay in line with your will, which is always best, then I'll do it. Keep me from complaining and from feeling bitterness towards you and the path you are leading me along. At the end of this hard season, there will be a blessing for me. Thank you for that promise!"

by Lisa Cheater

What's your color?

"Splendor and majesty are before Him, strength and joy are in His place." - **1 Chronicles 16:27**

Are you a winter or a spring? I'm not talking about fashion, I'm referring to your attitude, perspective, personality, and temperament. If you are walking closely with Me, your attitude will be full of golden joy, green hope, and orange zeal, even when problems surface. Today, pray for someone you know who seems stuck in the grey and blue of despair.

Now What? *Pray:* "Jesus, sometimes the person stuck in the blues of despair is me. Free me from disappointment and hurt, and bring to my mind another person who needs you to color their world with hope. If not in name, Lord, help me recognize anyone in my path today that needs a helpful comment, compliment, or pat on the back from me. Thank you for those people you place in my day who lift me up as well."

Blessed vacations . . .

"He restores my soul; He guides me in the paths of righteousness for His name's sake." - **Psalm 23:3**

Are you already dreaming about your next vacation, a chance to get away from all the pressure of your normal life and have some fun? Though traveling to beautiful places is exciting, you don't have to go to an exotic location or fancy hotel to return refreshed, renewed and reenergized. My Word can help you do that from any place—even your backyard! Commit this verse to memory as a reminder, an instant vacation for the soul, about how I am able to restore your faith and courage whenever you call upon Me in faith, in any season of your life.

Now what? *Pray:* "Jesus, restore my soul and lead me on the path of righteousness. Rebuild my courage for I am tired and overwhelmed. Right now, as I take a deep breath, may I remember these words whenever I need a time out or confirmation that you are always with me."

by Lisa Cheater

Not all prayers are the same . . .

"O Lord, it is You who made the Heaven and the earth and the sea, and all that is in them..." - **Acts 4:24**

It's tempting to think of Me as a giant Santa Claus, ready to grant your wishes for anything you want. But there is a model for your prayers if you want them to be heard and answered. First, PRAISE Me, for I live in words of gratitude. Second, CONFESS your sins that separate us so I can actually hear your prayer. Third, THANK Me for all I have done for you thus far. *Then*, ASK for what you need and for the needs of others. In this process, I am glorified and will hear your plea!

Now what? *Pray:* "Father, you are amazing, all-powerful, and the Bible tells me you are able to do more in my life than I have ever dared ask or think. Yes, I do sometimes think of you like a big cosmic genie who can fix my problems with the snap of a finger. Forgive my arrogance and pride, Lord! Thank you for always having my best interest in mind even if it means telling me, '*no*.' Help me remember to praise, confess, and thank you before I ask for something."

Know it all . . .

"The fear of the LORD is the beginning of wisdom, and the knowledge of the Holy One is understanding." - **Proverbs 9:10**

Life Situuation #4: Respect for God + Learning Scripture = Wisdom[10+]

> Now What? *Pray:* "Great are you, God, for you alone are the author of Truth. My academic studies are important, but so is your Word, which contains the wisdom for any crisis I will ever face, the answers for any question I have about living within your will. May I never stray from you, and may my life be a proving testimony of your power before others."

by Lisa Cheater

I am the ultimate judge . . .

"Never pay back evil for evil to anyone." - **Romans 12:17**

Why is being a Christian so hard? Because My way conflicts with the sin in the world. Your inclination is to fight back when someone is cruel to you, but I alone can see your opponent's whole life and can judge punishment. Self-control requires patience and practice, but the next time you are angry, resist the urge to retaliate in anger or violence. Trust that I know all about the situation and will bless you for obeying Me.

Now What? *Pray:* "Jesus, it blows my mind to know you can see the entire universe *and* every detail of my life—at once! As I mature and grow older I will see evidence of your justice, but for now, I must trust you. You are in control of my enemies even when it seems they are getting away with all kinds of wrongdoing. Oh, Lord, grant me self-control so that when I am threatened, I will not sin against you."

It all has a purpose ...

"And not only this, but we also exult in our tribulations, knowing that tribulation brings about perseverance; and perseverance, proven character; and proven character, hope." - **Romans 5:3-5**

Every event in your life, good and bad, has a role in shaping you into the person I created you to be. You may have all sorts of plans and dreams, but understand that any trouble you encounter has first been filtered through My hands. That may seem harsh because your goal is usually to avoid discomfort at all costs! But once you get through this difficult time (and you will), you'll become stronger, encouraged, and better equipped to handle the next challenge. I give you this teaching because I love you and know how much more you can be.

Now What? *Pray:* "Jesus, I must be in the middle of an awesome character-shaping experience because a huge trial that has been weighing heavy on my mind is: _____ (name it)_____. Lord, please remove this problem before me. But if is your will for me to go through it rather than around it, give me courage to persevere when things get really tough. My hope is in you, and I know you will bring good from this situation."

by Lisa Cheater

178

Hate is murder . . .

"You shall not murder." - **Exodus 20:13**

This commandment means more than simply not killing anyone. I want you to take hate from your heart. To Me, just thinking about how much you despise someone is just as bad as killing. Pray for those with whom you have conflicts, and read the Bible for insight into how to handle specific situations. Despite being in conflict with my teaching, hatred is a painful waste of time: the person you loathe feels none of your resentment, and the flaming anger in your heart burns only you.

Now What? *Pray:* "Jesus, forgive me for keeping hate and anger in my heart. It consumes me at times, and I lash out in ways that I know displease you, including hurting innocent people I love. Bind my instinct to react with harsh words. Replace my feelings of resentment and revenge with an attitude of peace and faith in you, for only you can bring good from bad situations, even relationships."

179

I am your army ...

"The LORD is my light and my salvation; Whom shall I fear? The LORD is the defense of my life; Whom shall I dread?" - **Psalms 27:1**

Who but God has the ability to place all the planets and stars in the sky? No one else in the history of the Universe can create a bird, an oak tree, water, or return from death! So then, don't be afraid of trying new things or managing a difficult challenge. The Creator of everything is on your side!

Now What? *Pray:* "Jesus, why do I spend any time worrying about things over which I have no control? I have no reason to fear anything or anyone for you are with me at all times. Walk with me through this day, and should I begin to doubt or feel afraid, bring this scripture to my mind, for YOU, Lord, *are* my light and my salvation, the defense of my life! Thank you for surrounding me with your amazing power."

by Lisa Cheater

Don't trash My house...

"...the body is not for immorality, but for the Lord..." -
1 Corinthians 6:13

You are My living body on earth! There are many temptations in the world, opportunities for pleasure and enjoyment, but I created your body to remain a holy place for Me to dwell. Don't contaminate My temple with sexual sin, drugs, or alcohol that can destroy your physical well-being and reputation. Is your body is a good place for Me to hang out? If not, tell Me about it, and let's clean house.

Now What? *Pray:* "Jesus, if I envision my body like a room, it'd probably be trashed. There's unconfessed sin on the floor, hidden secrets in the dresser drawers, and torn dreams in the corners. No thief came in and created that mess. I did it. Forgive me, Lord, for not valuing the life and body you have given me! Make me well and whole! Remove the junk, the bad habits, the addictions, the lack of attention. Beginning today, I will be mindful of what I consume, what I do, and what I see. May my whole being become more and more like you."

Suit up daily ...

"If anyone wishes to come after Me, he must deny himself, and take up his cross daily and follow Me." - **Luke 9:23**

Once you trust Me as your Savior, your place in Heaven is secure forever. Because the world is flawed, however, living out your salvation requires you to refocus your heart and mind upon me every day. Denying yourself and taking up your cross means you are willing to allow Me to dictate how you spend your time and money, no matter how much you want to do something else. In that commitment of selflessness, I will bless you abundantly.

Now What? *Pray:* "Lord, I am so glad you are more than a character in a book. You are a living, Holy God that wants to have a relationship with me! Lead my steps today. Show me the places you want me to go and how I should spend my time. Close doors I should avoid and open others that lead to opportunity. Though the world and its many disappointments may try to strip me of my faith and my confidence, I will trust you, Jesus, to lead the way."

by Lisa Cheater

Respond vs. react...

"Tremble, and do not sin; meditate in your heart upon your bed, and be still." - **Psalms 4:4**

Sometimes you get so angry your whole body shakes and your jaw clenches. When anger is used to defend the helpless or solve an injustice, it's a good thing, but don't allow your anger to cause you to sin by saying something disrespectful to your parents, hurting a friend, or wrecking someone's property. Those actions will only damage your Christian witness. Instead, pray about what's sending you through the roof, and seek My Word for understanding about how you should respond.

Now What? *Pray:* "Jesus, forgive me for my temper, for saying things out of emotion and fury without measuring their impact. I can choose how I respond to any infuriating situation; no one can *make* me mad. I choose it. When my chest feels like it will explode in anger, remind me of these words, that I should take time to cool down before I fly off the handle. Thank you for your perfect example of patience."

Wild things ...

"But these men revile the things which they do not understand; and the things which they know by instinct, like unreasoning animals, by these things they are destroyed." - **Jude 1:10**

My deepest desire is for all people to be saved, but a life of rebellion will lead to destruction. You already know people who approach each day like a wild animal, living by instinct and impulse. These people have a hard time understanding My teaching because their minds are clouded up with evil. You, my chosen, are not like them! Steer clear of the desire to say and do whatever you want, and accept My authority as evidence of My love for you.

Now What? *Pray:* "You, Jesus, are my strength, my shield, my light. I see now that when people put down my faith, my church, or talk evil against you, it's because they don't understand what it means to be a Christian. They don't hate me, they simply don't get it. Lord, soften the stony attitudes of the lost, and protect me from feelings of inferiority when I am confronted by their hurtful words. Thank you for loving me enough to provide a positive direction for my life!"

by Lisa Cheater

184

Celebrate dependence . . .

"So if the Son sets you free, you will be free indeed." - **John 8:36**

Americans celebrate their independence as a nation every July 4th, but remember that true freedom is found in knowing Me, not merely through a certain political system. Democracy gives you the ability to vote and determine laws that govern your land, but only I can grant personal freedom and joy that comes from knowing you don't *have* to sin. Do you see that? My death on the cross made a way for you to be liberated and forgiven from a lifetime of guilt and sadness. Choose Me. And be free!

Now what? *Pray:* "Father, thank you for the freedoms we enjoy in this country, the ability to pray and go to church and speak of you as my Lord. But mostly, I thank you for freeing me from a life condemned to sin. Because of you, I am free to love, free to forgive, free to choose right, and free to say no to wrong. I will be mindful today, Lord, of the joy I have in you."

You are a missionary ...

"Go therefore and make disciples of all the nations, baptizing them in the name of the Father and the Son and the Holy Spirit, teaching them to observe all that I commanded you; and lo, I am with you always, even to the end of the age." - **Matthew 28:19-20**

I never intended for you to keep Salvation to yourself. I want Believers to share what I've done for them with other people so that they, too, can be saved. Think about your friends and neighbors, people at school. Are some of them non-Believers? Live out your faith every day, invite them to church, and share how I've impacted your life. You are a living witness to My goodness with a unique story. Tell it!

Now What? *Pray:* "Jesus, you are the best thing that has ever happened to me, and yet I spend little-to-zero time telling others, even my closest friends, about your love and grace. Lord, give me a heart and mind that is sold-out for you! Teach me to use my online connections for more than posting pics and thoughts: it's a way to broadcast how mighty and good you are to me! Most of all, let my life be an open testimony of my commitment to you."

by Lisa Cheater

Let go of that grudge . . .

"...first be reconciled to your brother, and then come and present your offering." - **Matthew 5:24**

I love talking with you, and I am always listening for your voice, but if you carry a vendetta against a friend or family member and have unforgiveness in your heart, I cannot hear your prayers. Before you come to Me, go make the situation right with that person. Ask forgiveness if you need to. Then come to Me with a clear conscience and an open, obedient heart ready to be blessed.

Now What? *Pray:* "Lord, anger and bitterness feel like bowling balls hanging around my neck. They weigh me down and accomplish nothing. You already know I hold a grudge against ____(name person)____, and even though I feel justified in my resentment, I know my attitude grieves your heart. Forgive me, Lord, for holding onto my anger like a child's toy. I release my bitterness against this person, and from today on, I will no longer allow in thoughts of malice against them. Thank you for showing me mercy so I can show it to others."

Unload your heart ...

"Arise, cry aloud in the night ... Pour out your heart like water before the presence of the Lord." - **Lamentations 2:19**

Sometimes burdens are so heavy it's hard for you to lift your head. You want to crawl under your pillows and stay there for an eternity. Let Me take those problems from you! Pour out your heart to Me in prayer, unrestrained, like dumping water from a pitcher. Just let it all out and don't hold anything back! Cry if you need to! Once your heart is empty of sorrow, I can fill it up with My peace.

Now what? *Pray:* "Jesus, you are closer than my breath, and although I try to hold my feelings in, I cannot hide my emotions from you. I can be completely honest with you, knowing you won't abandon me for sharing my deepest fears and disappointments. Lord, I cannot bear these problems, but you can. As I pour them out to you, everything that hurts and scares me, calm me with your peace and confidence."

by Lisa Cheater

Seeing isn't believing ...

"And they came to Him and woke Him, saying, 'Save us, Lord; we are perishing!' He said to them, 'Why are you afraid, you men of little faith?' Then He got up and rebuked the winds and the sea, and it became perfectly calm." - **Matthew 8:25-26**

Would it really be easier to rely on Me if I was physically on the earth, where you could see and touch Me? Don't forget, I've been there. I *did* walk beside real men, women, and children, and many *still* didn't believe in Me. I was right there! Even My closest disciples would freak out in moments of doubt! Although you can't see Me, I am there, next to you right now at school, throughout the night, when driving, on dates, or in a busy crowd. There's no reason to cower during the life's storms.

Now what? *Pray:* "Lord, though I cannot see you with my eyes, I know you are real. I can feel your quiet peace, I marvel at the creation you have made, I can witness the amazing miracles (small and large) you perform, and I can sense your presence when I worship with other Believers. One day I will see you as others saw you on earth. Until then, increase my ability to see how you are working in my life every day."

189

Positive talk . . .

"...There must be no filthiness and silly talk, or coarse jesting, which are not fitting, but rather giving of thanks." - **Ephesians 5:4**

Non-believers are constantly watching you and other Christians to see if you're for real. They are just waiting to call you a hypocrite or challenge your faith, and one of the easiest ways to judge you is by what you say. If you tease others, tell nasty jokes, laugh at profanity, and swear, the world will consider your religion worthless. Worse still, someone may choose NOT to believe in Me because of your actions. Use kind words that build up others. People will notice that, too.

Now what? *Pray:* "Jesus, I love being admired and in the center of attention. I love to make others laugh and smile though sometimes it's at someone else's expense. Allow me to put myself in someone else's place when I feel like poking fun at them. I don't like being embarrassed, and I need courage to step in and defend someone who is being humiliated. I would want someone to do that for me! May the attention and admiration I desire come from doing the right thing."

by Lisa Cheater

Wittle Chwistians . . .

"For God has not given us a spirit of timidity, but of power and love and discipline." - **2 Timothy 1:7**

Come on, what's your *real* opinion of Christians? Placid, meek, mild, square, boring, lame, passive? If My teachings seem like this to you, go back to the cross. Death itself was defeated by My power! Nothing hushes an irate person like love and self-control! People change the way they live their lives because of the joy they see in a Believer. THAT is serious power! Practice the Fruits of the Spirit today and see what happens.

BTW: Remember, the Fruits of the Spirit are love, joy, peace, patience, kindness, goodness, faithfulness, gentleness, and self-control. (Galatians 5:22)

Now what? *Pray:* "Lord, when I picture you I see quiet, controlled strength that is always right and just. You are my example! Place in me the fruits of your Spirit so I can grow in my faith and as a witness to your power. Thank you, Jesus, for your clear Word. I don't have to wonder what is "right" behavior; what you expect of me is all in the Bible. And though I am not perfect, I *am* forgiven."

191

Keys to success . . .

"Hate evil, you who love the LORD, Who preserves the souls of His godly ones; He delivers them from the hand of the wicked."- **Psalms 97:10**

As you move through each day, make a conscious effort to avoid the temptation of trying different pleasures as an escape from life. I am your Deliverer in times of trouble. If you seek My Father's plan for your life rather than just doing things your way, I will protect and guard you through every struggle. It might not always be a breeze, but I will always steer you away from danger.

Now what? *Pray:* "Jesus, you are always the perfect source of direction and comfort. Some people drink, eat or listen to music when they are stressed. My usual response to anxiety is to: ____(name it)____. The temptations around me are enticing, sweet, glittery, shiny and cool, but today when I become frazzled, help me run first to you instead of things (or other people, or chocolate, or alcohol, etc.). Keep me within your plan, even when I can't clearly see the way."

by Lisa Cheater

192

Be courageous ...

"I command you – be strong and courageous! Do not be afraid or discouraged. For the LORD your God is with you wherever you go." -
Joshua 1:9

Courage is not the absence of fear. Courage means you are willing to do something even though you ARE afraid. I have given you specific skills for a reason, and at times I will challenge you with situations that you might find overwhelming at first. My strength is most evident during times of your weakness!

Now what? *Pray:* "Jesus, sometimes I feel like one of the ducks on a shelf at a shooting gallery. People and situations seem to be taking turns firing at me, one right after another! But rather that falling over in defeat, help me stand firm under fire and to face terrifying situations with courage, for YOU are in control of everything."

Toss out your good-o-meter ...

"For all have sinned and fall short of the glory of God..." - **Romans 3:23**

Not some, *all*. No one is good enough to be in the presence of Most High God, which is exactly why I died, to become the bridge of forgiveness. But resist the tendency to compare yourself to other Christians. Things aren't always as they appear. You cannot judge your interior against someone else's exterior. You never know how another person might be struggling at home or in private. Focus on your relationship with Me, and remember that I didn't come for saints; I came for sinners!

Now what? *Pray:* "Jesus, thank you for giving your life and for your amazing grace. I know I am supposed to try to live out your teachings and example every day, though I will not be perfect. And yet you love me just as much when I stumble as when I am victorious. Lord, I will not compare my talents, blessings, gifts, or spiritual maturity against another Christian for you have designed me exactly the way you want, faults and all."

by Lisa Cheater

The ultimate stain lifter!

"Be gracious to me, O God, according to Your loving-kindness; according to the greatness of Your compassion blot out my transgressions." - **Psalms 51:1**

Every carpet has at least one stain that won't come out. No matter what you spray on it, that stubborn stain seems part of the carpet fiber itself. Imagine a spray that will instantly remove that spot, even if it's been there for years. I can do that in your life! When you truly repent of your sins by confessing them to Me and asking for forgiveness, determined to not repeat it, I remove the stain in your heart and make your life spotless. No matter what you are struggling with, I can cleanse your life. Guaranteed.

Now what? *Pray:* "Jesus, forgive me today for the sins I have committed against you, those I am very aware of, and even those I've overlooked. Be merciful to me, Father, and wipe away the stains of guilt, self-hatred, and confusion from my heart. Cleanse me from the inside out, and fill me with your joy and comforting peace. Thank you for restoring my faith today."

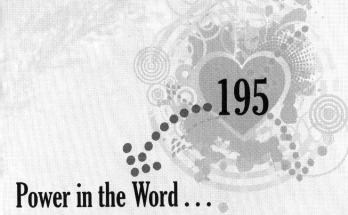

Power in the Word ...

"For the Word of God is living and active and sharper than any two-edged sword, and piercing as far as the division of soul and spirit, of both joints and marrow, and able to judge the thoughts and intentions of the heart." - **Hebrews 4:12**

The Bible is more than a book of ancient history and fantasy stories. It is the inspired word of God, and its truths are proven and indisputable. Even many non-Christians have a hard time arguing against scripture! Sometimes a specific verse will remind you how much God loves you or convict you of wrong behavior. The Bible provides wisdom and can change how you feel. No other book contains that kind of power!

Now what? *Pray:* "Lord, thank you for your awesome Word in scripture! It's amazing how words written hundreds, sometimes thousands, of years ago still ring true today. It proves to me that you see all of time at once and that scripture is trustworthy. Etch your words in my mind, and especially help me remember verses that 'hit me between the eyes'. I will look out for those verses, seek them with all my heart, every time I read the Bible, for they are your specific messages to me."

by Lisa Cheater

Forgiveness leads to gratefulness . . .

"I will give thanks to You, O LORD; For although You were angry with me, Your anger is turned away, and You comfort me." - **Isaiah 12:1**

One role of your parents is to guide you away from choices that lead to certain destruction. When you oppose them, you get into serious trouble, often with stiff consequences. Likewise, the anger of God is fierce, yet when you ask forgiveness and turn from your rebellion, God will comfort you, just like a loving parent. Believe it or not, as you get older you will be grateful for tough, loving correction.

Now what? *Pray:* "Jesus, the pain of punishment that comes from my sin is second only to knowing I have disappointed you. Dealing with consequences when I mess up is awful, and though I complain, I know you allow me to face these experiences because you care so much about me and want the best life for me. Thank you, Jesus, for caring about who I am and where I'm heading. Be always near me, Lord."

197

Set free . . .

"Rid yourselves of all the offenses you have committed, and get a new heart and a new spirit." - **Ezekiel 18:31 (NIV)**

I know you desire to live for Me, even though your world makes that mission very difficult. Don't become discouraged if you falter in your Christian walk! You don't need to drag your faults around like a ball and chain. Acknowledge where you have stumbled, and allow Me to replace sin with loving guidance over your life. You will not be able to "be good" on your own. Daily, ask Me for the strength to you'll need to avoid temptation and love others.

> Now what? *Pray:* "Lord, you know I have repeat offenses, areas of my life that I struggle with regularly, and yet nearly every sin is tied to one: selfishness. Today, my prayer is that you would break me out of the habit of selfishness, and let me make time to care for the needs and interests of others. Give me a new attitude, a new heart that beats like yours."

by Lisa Cheater

What is faith anyway?

"Now faith is being sure of what we hope for and certain of what we do not see." - **Hebrews 11:1 (NIV)**

Some describe faith as merely a belief in something, but it's much bigger than that. You've never seen Me with your own eyes, right? Yet you believe in Me. You trust scriptures that tell you about My life, death and resurrection, the accounts of witnesses who saw Me ascend into Heaven. Although My disciple Thomas wanted evidence of My identity after My resurrection, I show special favor to those who believe without the benefit of physical proof.

Now what? *Pray:* "Father, I believe in you with all my heart, soul, and mind because of what I've seen and felt you do in my life. Your Word says that every blessing, every good thing, is a gift from you, and I can feel your presence in my mind and heart. You calm me when I am afraid, you strengthen me when I feel tired, and you open doors that shape my future. I believe because everything you lived and died for hinges around love that changes people, including me! Thank you, Lord, for sending the Holy Spirit to be with me until I meet you face to face."

Not just for adults ...

"You shall not commit adultery." - **Exodus 20:14**

Quite simply, adultery is having a sexual relationship with someone outside of marriage. Why do I tell you this now? Because the media and movies constantly illustrate the opposite of what is right. Film characters and celebrities are in and out of so many different beds, it's hard for the paparazzi to keep up. When you read these stories or see them played out in a movie, know that this behavior is directly against My Father's commandment. It's not ok.

Now what? *Pray:* "Jesus, I see so much promiscuity that I barely notice it. Your words remind me how far from your will we, as a world of people, have fallen. God, keep me pure, throughout my life, and protect me from the temptation of adultery. Raise up my generation to boldly proclaim a faithful commitment to marriage."

by Lisa Cheater

Your safe place . . .

"The LORD is my rock and my fortress and my deliverer, my God, my rock, in whom I take refuge; my shield and the horn of my salvation, my stronghold." - **Psalms 18:2**

There's something special about hiding places. Play forts, the space under the bed, the closet...they are all places where you felt protected and hidden as a child. Even animals hide in a hole or den to get away from danger. Don't try to fight your battles alone and exposed. I am your fortress, your safe place! Whenever you feel afraid or confused, run to Me and let Me cover you with My blanket of protection.

Now what? *Pray:* "Lord, why do I freak out when things don't go my way? How can I doubt your strength? You created everything, including me! Like the medieval castles I learned about in history, you are my fortress and my shelter in any kind of battle. Help me remember to run to you in good times and in bad. Today, I will make you my first stop for every need."

Stronger than Super Glue . . .

"Who will separate us from the love of Christ? Will tribulation, or distress, or persecution, or famine, or nakedness, or peril, or sword?"- **Romans 8:35**

There is nothing - *nothing* - that can separate us. Sometimes you forget that I am with you and your focus and confidence begin to shake. Never doubt that I am with you always. Do this: the next time you go to the mountains or the beach, choose a shell or small stone, one that really jumps out at you for some reason. Write My name on it and keep it in your pocket, backpack, or purse as a reminder that you are in My sight at all times.

Now what? *Pray:* "Lord, so many of my relationships are conditional; if I mess up once or say something wrong, some of my friends will drop me like a hot potato. I am so thankful that you are not like that. No matter how many times I let my tongue slip, or fall outside your will for my life, you are always there waiting for me. My salvation is secure, and I never have to worry about being good enough; because of your merciful love, I am."

by Lisa Cheater

The heart's speaker ...

"...For the mouth speaks out of that which fills the heart." - **Matthew 12:34**

Does your conduct at school *and* at home and line up with your claim to be a Christian? Some may claim to know Me as their Lord and Savior, but evidence of my leadership is not visible in their life. If I am truly in someone's heart, his words and behavior will reflect that commitment. Does your behavior show you love Me?

Now what? *Pray:* "Search me, Oh, Lord, and show me where my speech is displeasing to you. Are my words sassy or constantly filled with anger? Do I litter my sentences with curses? Are my comments hurtful to others instead of helpful? God, it takes so much self-control to bridle what I say! Filter the words that come out of my mouth. May they prove my commitment to live for you and as you did, speaking only with truth, love, and selflessness."

203

Promise carefully . . .

"[Hannah, Samson's mother] said, 'O LORD of hosts, if You will indeed...give Your maidservant a son, then I will give him to the LORD all the days of his life, and a razor shall never come on his head.'" - **1 Samuel 1:11**

There's no need to bargain with Me when you are in the middle of a crisis. You don't need to promise Me some trinket or "better behavior" for Me to hear your prayer, otherwise, like Hannah, you might end up having to deliver on a promise over which you have no control. Instead, confess the areas of life where you struggle most, and trust Me completely with the process of reshaping your will.

> Now what? *Pray:* "Lord, thank you for loving me without expectation or condition. You know I am learning. You know I am trying. The area of my life I have the hardest time giving over to you is ____(name it)_____. Take this part of me, Lord, and make your plans mine, whatever that entails. Help me resist the urge to take over and do things myself, my way."

by Lisa Cheater

Love vs. guilt . . .

"I do not write these things to shame you, but to admonish you as my beloved children." - **1 Corinthians 4:14**

Do My commandments make you feel secure or guilty? Satan will often try to convince you that you're a failure and that following Me is impossible. Run from those lies and put them out of your mind! Because I love you, I will not allow you to drift along life's uncertain current. My way flows to absolute truth, eternal life, genuine friendship, and an abundant life. You are not being punished; you are being loved.

Now what? *Pray:* "Jesus, you are perfect, unshakable, and your love is true and right. Always! Your teachings are not merely rules and commandments set for the sake of controlling me, they are indisputable guides that will keep my life on track throughout my whole life. No other god is above your ways. No other self-help plan or motivational theory can stand up against you! Thank you for your loving discipline."

Einstein on steroids...

"Behold, the fear of the Lord is wisdom; and to depart from evil is understanding." - **Job 28:28**

You can be as brilliant as the world's most famous mathematician, but only My Holy Spirit can develop wise character. Those who are truly wise have a healthy fear of My power and authority, just as you'd have respect for a loving parent or admired teacher. Doing your best in school is extremely important, but only reverence for Me can help you know the right way to handle people, situations, and difficulties. The combination of the two is genuine wisdom!

> Now what? *Pray:* "Jesus, I long for true wisdom. I long for the day when I can walk away from temptations with courage, knowing I have been victorious in battle against the enemy. Your process of teaching me how to be like you is unique to me; no one else receives the lessons you've written for me. Today, when I encounter difficult people or situations, help me apply all I have learned about you and your ways. May I pause to meet each challenge by asking myself: *'Jesus, what would you do?'*"

by Lisa Cheater

Skills need exercise . . .

"Do not neglect the spiritual gift within you..." - **1 Timothy 4:14**

I have given every Believer at least one specific talent such as music, leadership, organization, teaching, taking care of others, encouraging friends, learning languages, telling people about Me, and many others. You know where you excel - think about it! My intent is for you use these gifts in Christian service to lead others to Me. Stop burying your abilities beneath busyness, and don't wait for someone else to do the work I've put on your heart. You are smarter than that! Get busy using the skills I've entrusted to only you.

Now what? *Pray:* "Jesus, I get so busy in everyday life that I forget that I have any skills at all! Yes, you have gifted me with talents. I know I am skilled in _____ (name skill(s)_____. How can I use this ability to strengthen your kingdom? How can I help lead lost people to you or strengthen the faith of other Christians? I'm wide open to your will! Just show me the way."

Ultimate thirst quencher ...

"Jesus answered and said to her, '...whoever drinks of the water that I will give him shall never thirst...'" - **John 4:13-14**

There is nothing better than a huge glass of ice water on a sweltering summer day. Not even Gatorade will quench your thirst like plain water. I am like a glass of cold water when you are about to collapse from the burning pressure of life. You might try other things to relieve your need and pain, but nothing will restore and refresh your spirit like me! Have confidence in Me. You will never be satisfied by another substitute.

Now what? *Pray:* "Jesus, all too often I try to fill my needs with things other than you. The feeling is complete and utter dissatisfaction. Just like the woman at the well, I don't want any substitute for real joy and forgiveness. Only you will do. Instead of running to some cheap replacement that is rarely good for me and usually only delays my pain, I will run to you first in prayer."

by Lisa Cheater

A perfect prayer...

"I wait for the LORD, my soul does wait, and in His word do I hope."-
Psalms 130:5

I see all the issues that press in on you from every side like a trash compactor. Learning to be independent and self-reliant as a young adult can be frightening. Fear of the unknown or rejection makes you sharp and impatient with yourself and others, especially when you don't know what to do. So as you mature and become more independent, become more dependent upon Me! Just take a deep breath and trust My promises to take care of all your worries as you wait for answers.

Now what? *Pray:* "Lord, I hate waiting, but I know I cannot rush your timing or your plan which are always, *always*, perfect. I'm at peace when I see your will and your plans for me unfolding. It's the space in between, where I am waiting on your guidance, that I really flounder and need your support. Teach me to pray when I am afraid, to wait with patience, and to seek answers in scripture when I am confused."

Ok, when you say everything . . .

"In everything give thanks; for this is God's will for you in Christ Jesus." - **1 Thessalonians 5:18**

Voicing gratitude in good times often slips your mind, but to be thankful for *problems*? No way! You wonder what kind of God would even make difficulties part of His plan for you! According to the world's standards that may seem unfair, but just think about someone you know who has gone through a crisis and come out of it stronger and more pumped to share the Gospel than before. Transformation is definitely something for which to be thankful!

Now what? *Pray:* "Lord, though I may not always feel gratitude, especially for problems, I will praise you in all things. When people I think are my friends desert me, I will thank you for protection. When a storm hits my party, I will be grateful for the rain. If I'm not accepted to my college or job choice, I will praise you for closing doors that lead me to your path. In all circumstances, help me find the bright, God-filled spot."

by Lisa Cheater

Unplug ...

"When Elijah heard [the sound of a gentle wind], he wrapped his face in his mantle and went out and stood in the entrance of a cave. And behold, a voice came to him and said, 'What are you doing here, Elijah?'" - **1 Kings 19:13**

You occasionally strain to hear My voice, but I won't compete with your television, computer games, cell phone, and iPod. You are so busy filling your day with noise to make yourself feel good, you forget where I can be found: in the quiet. I don't shout through a cosmic megaphone, I whisper. Be still and totally quiet with the Bible, My words. Pick a verse and listen. Then, you'll be able to hear Me.

Now what? *Pray:* "Lord, as I move through this day, allow me to find one quiet place where I can just sit and listen. No phone, no music. Just you and me. Clear my thoughts of all my troubles and anxieties, the junk that's already accumulated today, and let your voice come to me just like it did for Elijah! I need to hear you, Jesus."

Eeeew, cockroaches ...

"For everyone who does evil hates the Light, and does not come to the Light for fear that his deeds will be exposed." - **John 3:20**

Ever wonder why crimes mostly take place at night? To avoid getting caught. The daylight makes it too easy for cops to spot a criminal up to no good. Even cockroaches run into a dark corner when a light is turned on. Non-Believers criticize My teaching (and even you) because they don't want to be near the Truth. The darkness in their life rebels against My goodness because I am The Light of the World!

Now what? *Pray:* "Lord God, protect me against people who love to dwell in the darkness, and stir in my heart with warnings when I am near evil. Steer me (and my life) towards others who know you as their Savior and love the light. May I never be ashamed for your light to shine on my life. Without secrets, deceit, or lies, I lay myself as an open book before you."

by Lisa Cheater

Right way . . .

"Teach me to do your will, for you are my God; may your good Spirit lead me on level ground." - **Psalms 143:10 (NIV)**

Life Situquation #5: Surrender + Obedience = Direction

Now what? *Pray:* "Jesus, though the world tries to tell me I am ultimately in control of my future, I know I am not, nor do I want to be! I'll only mess it up. Help me see that surrender doesn't mean giving in, it means letting you have control, the one who knows best. It's like floating down a calm, swift-moving river, allowing it to carry me to the destination. Instead of fighting the current, I will let you carry me wherever you want to take me."

Bad and the good ...

"All things came into being through Him..." - **John 1:3**

How can a kind and generous God allow murder, war, natural disasters, and bad things to happen to good people? I'm not blind to the suffering in your world, the ill effects of sin and hate, but I did not create you to be a robot. I give everyone the ability to *choose* Me over a life of sin. Many of the bad things that happen are the results of poor choices, but even when the innocent are caught in the crossfire, I am there and able to bring good from any evil.

Now what? *Pray:* "Lord, things happen every week that seem so unfair, but I choose to believe your Word and your promise that you can make good come out of every bad situation for those that love you. If my friends choose immorality, I will choose you. If my plans fall into a million pieces, I will choose you. And when I am so down that I can't lift my head, I will choose you. Thank you Jesus, for righteousness that never, ever fails."

by Lisa Cheater

The rocking chair . . .

"And who of you by being worried can add a single hour to his life?" - **Matthew 6:27**

Like sitting in a rocking chair, worry gives you something to do, but it doesn't get you very far. You spend so much time fretting and wondering about problems. It keeps you up at night and makes your stomach turn. Has it helped? No! Many of your worries are beyond your control, so stop obsessing about things that may never even happen! Give Me your concerns, and trust Me to lead you, one day at a time.

Now what? *Pray:* "Lord, you are my peace of mind and my shelter. Thank you for taking all my concerns, especially those I cannot control, and working them out for me. Right now, I am most worried about: ____(name it)____. Prevent my thoughts from drifting into anxiety, and lead me to the right decisions and actions. I will not fret! You hold me and my problems in your hand."

The Lord's fire extinguisher . . .

"A gentle answer turns away wrath, but a harsh word stirs up anger."-
Proverbs 15:1

A funny thing happens when you respond quietly to someone who is up in your grill. When you respond with a very gentle word instead of screaming back, your assailant is forced to hush in order to hear what you're saying. It confuses them! Remember this the next time someone wants to go a round with you, to make you as mad as they are. Your self-control will extinguish the argument.

Now what? *Pray:* "I'll need your help with this one, Lord. My goal in an argument is to be heard! It's so hard for me to believe that responding quietly will work, but because you say it's so, I will try. The next time someone starts screaming at me, help me respond in control and with a soft voice. If they don't calm down, I will turn and walk away instead of stooping to their level and yelling back."

by Lisa Cheater

Proof in the power . . .

"Do not be afraid. Stand firm and you will see the deliverance the LORD will bring you today." - **Exodus 14:13**

Each year, your life changes. New class at school, new friends, new challenges. Sometimes, you wish everything would just stay the same where life is comfortable and predictable, but then you would never grow up. Obstacles prepare you to handle bigger things, and I am with you through each one of them just as I stood beside Moses in Egypt. Face change with courage because I never leave your side!

Now what? *Pray:* "Jesus, yes, change makes me nervous because it forces me to adapt, to change myself, and to try different things outside my comfort zone. But I am so grateful that you never change. No matter where I travel, what school I attend, where I work, or who's with me, YOU are here to help me. You are my constant, always reliable, best friend."

217

Big faith?

"And the Lord said, 'If you had faith like a mustard seed, you would say to this mulberry tree, be uprooted and be planted in the sea; and it would obey you.'" - **Luke 17:6**

Accessing My power doesn't require Moses-like faith, just a small amount will do, like the size of a mustard seed. How big is that? About the size of a pin head or the tip of a sharp pencil. That's all. Do you have that much faith in Me to handle your darkest fears and deepest worries? Give it a try. Demonstrate your faith by not worrying about those fears and concerns anymore.

Now what? *Pray:* "Jesus, allow me to envision faith like taking a broken watch to a jeweler. I can take the watch to someone who knows how to fix the watch, but I won't worry about *how* it's being fixed, my job is simply to trust the workman and wait for the call when it's ready to be picked up. You are the master jeweler of my life, able to repair any situation I leave with you. Thank you, Lord, for your love. I will trust your awesome workmanship."

by Lisa Cheater

WWJD?

"Let all bitterness and wrath and anger and clamor and slander be put away from you, along with all malice. Be kind to one another, tender-hearted, forgiving each other, just as God in Christ also has forgiven you." - **Ephesians 4:31-32**

How many times should you forgive the person who has hurt you? Two times? Three? How many times should I forgive you? I pardon you on a daily basis, many times without you asking for it. That's called grace. Without Me, you are not able to show that level of kindness to another human being. When faced with the temptation to snap back in anger, stop for a moment and ask yourself how I would respond in that situation.

Now what? *Pray:* "Jesus, many people in my life are wonderful blessings. There are also people who drive me completely nuts that I'd like to eject from the globe. Some are blind to your goodness, others don't mean to be hurtful, they are simply learning to live your way, just like me. Give me your eyes, so that I might see others as fellow learners of your truth and support them in the same way I need encouragement."

219

This, too, will pass . . .

"He will yet fill your mouth with laughter and your lips with shouting."-
Job 8:21

"When will this stress go away? What did I do to deserve this?"
I often hear you ask these questions whenever trouble comes your way.
Problems can pile up and bog you down in depression if you let them,
but you must refuse the urge to harm yourself as a way to cope. Hard
times teach you to recognize My voice among all the other noise in your
life. One day you will look back on your current struggle and see how I
taught you through it.

Now what? *Pray:* "Jesus, you see every part of me,
behind the masked smiles I put on for others, beneath my
armor of happiness that hides a broken heart. You know
how I wrestle with becoming tangled in my worries
when I can't seem to get beyond them. Fill my heart with
assurance that these problems are temporary; they will
end at some point, one way or another, in your perfect
plan. Until then, hold my hand as we push through them
together."

by Lisa Cheater

Be healed . . .

"And [Jesus] stretched out His hand and touched [the leper], saying, 'I am willing; be cleansed.' And immediately the leprosy left him." - **Luke 5:13**

This very sick man asked Me one day if I would be *willing* to heal him of a disease. He knew I was able, but he first asked if it was My *will.* I was so touched, that yes, I healed him immediately. Not every answer to your prayers will be a "yes," but I will always, *always* do what is the very best for your life. If you first ask for My will, you will never be disappointed with the answer.

Now what? *Pray:* "Jesus, though I have many things to ask for, I will put them aside today to ask this one thing: for your plans to take over mine. Whatever path you send me on, Lord, I will go. Whatever you require me to say, I will speak it. Whatever you want me to do, I will do, even if it's not what I had hoped for. I am willing to give up my plan, for I know that when you direct my path, I WILL find joy."

221

Five finger discount . . .

"You shall not steal." - **Exodus 20:15**

Stealing breaks one of My fundamental commandments, yet there are more ways to pilfer than swiping money from your mom's wallet or a camera from a store. Cheating on a test, flirting with someone else's boyfriend or girlfriend, snatching a flower from someone's garden, or hacking into a computer are all forms of stealing. Theft shows your lack of trust in Me. I'll provide all you need! There's never a reason to rob someone else.

Now what? *Pray:* "Lord, you are my provider and the source from whom all my blessings come! Forgive me for the times I have taken something, whether small or large, that didn't belong to me. May I never be tempted again by this sin! I will trust you for the things I need and for all the little extras. I will honor you with hard work and respect for other people's stuff. Thank you, Jesus, for everything you have given me."

by Lisa Cheater

Choose your weapon . . .

"The weapons we fight with are not the weapons of the world. On the contrary, they have divine power to demolish strongholds." - **2 Corinthians 10:4 (NIV)**

A complete arsenal of weapons is at your disposal to bring down any argument and destroy the walls that Satan builds around people to keep them from knowing Me. Instead of arguing and fighting with people who seem lost and unreachable, use the spiritual armaments that I provide: faith, prayer, hope, unconditional love, and My Word, the Bible. These are the tools of victory!

Now what? *Pray:* "Jesus, with you at my side, I do not have to play the role of victim. You have equipped me to be a mighty warrior, with tools of Truth that can knock out any enemy! Though I am young, my honest and heartfelt prayers are more powerful than any of the enemy's schemes. When the world tries to crush me, I will reach for my sword—the Bible—and reconnect with your promises. Thank you, Lord, for your amazing, loving power!"

Word obsession . . .

"...like newborn babies, long for the pure milk of the word, so that by it you may grow in respect to salvation..." - **1 Peter 2:1-2**

Babies are insatiable when they're hungry. Nothing will satisfy an infant when he cries for a bottle. That is exactly the attitude that's needed if you desire to grow as a Christian. Hunger for the Truth of scripture so that nothing else will do! Spiritual maturity happens when you begin to consult and rely upon what the Bible says about every situation you face. The more you read, the more you learn, and the more like Me you'll become.

Now what? *Pray:* "Jesus, as I move through this day, mold my attitude to be like yours. May my soul hunger for the Truth of your Word. Bless me with knowledge as I study scripture and hear your teaching so that as I look more closely at you, I will become more like you. Remind me to always seek you and the Bible as balms for my troubled soul."

by Lisa Cheater

Do vs. Done...

"... a man is not justified by the works of the Law but through faith in Christ Jesus..." - **Galatians 2:16**

Here, Paul is talking about obeying God's Law, The Ten Commandments, and although it's important to obey them, doing so doesn't guarantee your spot in Heaven. It's not possible for anyone to keep all ten for their whole life! Only by accepting the grace of my death on the cross as payment for your sin and striving to live a life that follows My teachings, are you saved. Learn and remember those top ten commandments, though, for they guide your behavior, keep you safe, protect your relationships, and strengthen your faith in Me.

Now what? *Pray:* "Jesus, thank you for dying for me so that I don't have to feel guilty for all my imperfections and failures. Because of you, I have the assurance of Salvation. Not a *hope. Assurance!* As I grow as Christian, let these basic commandments from Exodus 20 be part of each day's goals: I will worship *only* God (not possessions or other people), I will use only words that glorify you, I will go to church regularly, I will obey my parents, I will not kill or hate, I will keep my thoughts pure, and I will tell the truth always."

Personal hero . . .

"I call upon the LORD, who is worthy to be praised, and I am saved from my enemies." - **Psalms 18:3**

You have many options to deal with malicious attacks against you or your integrity: anger, denial, depression, revenge, alcohol, drugs, eating disorders... Satan is just waiting for you to reach out for one of his tools of destruction. Reach to Me instead. I alone can save you from yourself, your enemies, and sin. History provides a proven record of My promise to rescue My people in times of trouble, so whenever you're distressed, call out for the only sure fix: Me.

Now what? *Pray:* "Lord, my enemies spear me with hurtful words and sometimes lie against me. Worst of all, they seem able to successfully deceive others while I am left behind. Protect me, Lord, from their callous assaults. If my life is pleasing to you, I have nothing to fear or feel guilty about. I will hold my head high and not be bothered! Let truth prevail, and may those who are intent upon hurting me learn to hold their tongues. Thank you for being my rescuer."

by Lisa Cheater

Is it real love?

"Love is patient, love is kind and is not jealous; love does not brag and is not arrogant, does not act unbecomingly; it does not seek its own, is not provoked, does not take into account a wrong suffered, does not rejoice in unrighteousness, but rejoices with the truth; bears all things, believes all things, hopes all things, endures all things." - **1 Corinthians 13:4-7**

You are at an age where the mystery of love and romance hangs around your head *alot*. They're pretty new feelings and often super confusing. You wonder how you're supposed to act around someone you like, and how to know if they really like you. This scripture is My definition of genuine love. Use it as your measuring stick against relationships as you mature and begin dating or making new friends.

Now what? *Pray:* "Jesus, in your face I see the perfect picture of love. You are patient and kind to me, you always rejoice in goodness, and you endure my selfishness with amazing grace and faithfulness. Change me to love the way you do, and lead me to those who hold to this same standard of devotion. Every true friend you send me is indeed a gift."

227

Some cheese to go with that whine?

"Do all things without grumbling or disputing; so that you will prove yourselves to be blameless and innocent, children of God above reproach in the midst of a crooked and perverse generation, among whom you appear as lights in the world..." - **Philippians 2:14-15**

If you could hear what I hear and see what I see on a daily basis, it would shock you. So many people, teens and adults, choose to whine and complain about everything! The weather, chores, lack of "stuff," too much "stuff," assignments, politics, the world in general... Because you are set apart as My child, My follower, you are to be a light, a bright spot in a world full of darkness and deceit. Don't fuel the negativity! Instead, shock your friends by telling them about the blessings in your life.

Now what? *Pray:* "Jesus, you are the Master Planner, and I trust you with every detail of my life. Who am I to gripe about anything when every day is a blessing? Lord, one thing I tend to complain about consistently is: ____(name it)____ . But instead of focusing on negatives today, train me to think of at least three positive things about every challenge or task. I may not like the rain, but it makes the plants grow, it cleans the air, and it produces rainbows. Fix my eyes upon the rainbows of each situation I face today."

by Lisa Cheater

The view at the top . . .

"Blessed is a man who perseveres under trial; for once he has been approved, he will receive the crown of life which the Lord has promised to those who love Him." - **James 1:12**

Think about your favorite vacations: a mountain climb, a swim out to the reef, awesome rides at the amusement park...and the excruciatingly long ride in the car to get there. The journey seemed an eternity, but the payoff was at the destination! Don't give up in the struggle you now face. The process, the journey, seems like it will never end, but it will, and when you get there, the reward for your perseverance will be worth the temporary discomfort! Remember, the awesome view at the top of the mountain is reserved for those who dare to climb.

Now what? *Pray:* "Lord, there are times in life when I seriously want to pull off at the next gas station, have a soda, and forget the destination. The journey seems too hard, too long, and I lose my will to press on through hardships. When I feel like giving up, Jesus, lift me to my feet and encourage me with counsel from my Christian friends and leaders. Flood my exhausted soul with courage and strength to finish the tasks I've begun."

Back on the cross ...

"For if we go on sinning willfully after receiving the knowledge of the truth, there no longer remains a sacrifice for sins..." - **Hebrews 10:26**

You learn more about My Way each time you read scripture or talk to Me in prayer. With the help of the Holy Spirit, you may even have a pretty solid idea about what is right and what is wrong in My view. I know you're not perfect, but each time you continue to sin, often repeating the same sin over and over, you hang Me back on the cross, and My death becomes meaningless. Honor my sacrifice for you by learning from your mistakes.

Now what? *Pray:* "Jesus, forgive me for purposefully doing things I know are wrong. You bring Truth to me through scripture, my parents, my church leaders, and authorities, and yet I still demand to do things my way. You died so I would be free to choose to live a life without sin! I don't have to attend every argument, every fight, and every temptation I'm invited to! Thank you, Jesus, for the power you give me to deny evil. Today, guide me with right decisions."

by Lisa Cheater

230

Be choosy . . .

"Do not be bound together with unbelievers; for what partnership have righteousness and lawlessness, or what fellowship has light with darkness?" - **2 Corinthians 6:14**

I want you to share the Gospel with non-Believers, but don't let yourself become *bound* to them. In other words, avoid dating, marrying, or going into a business partnership with someone who is not a genuine Christian. You will know by their fruit, their words, deeds, and speech, if they are My true follower. Pray for them, and do not judge, but don't allow them the chance to bring your standards down. You cannot change others; that's My job.

Now what? *Pray:* "Lord, search my slate of friends and impress upon my heart the name of anyone I have bound myself to who is not a genuine Believer. Give me the words and skills to place boundaries upon this relationship, and release me from any unhealthy ties that I have created with this person. Forgive me for launching ahead of you in my connections with others. May wisdom be my guide when meeting people and developing alliances from now on."

Come home . . .

"So he got up and came to his father. But while he was still a long way off, his father saw him and felt compassion for him, and ran and embraced him and kissed him." - **Luke 15:20**

The key to this story is in the first four words: "So he got up..." This young man left home to go do whatever he wanted, but the thrill of living wild quickly faded, and he finally came to his senses. Exhausted from all the partying and shallow relationships, the man decided to go home where it was safe. His father was waiting. Likewise, I will not force you to stay connected to Me, but I will always be here when you return. Just remember you can spare yourself a hard lesson by not leaving My side in the first place!

Now what? *Pray:* "Lord, my human nature makes me prone to wander and easily tempted by the shiny, bright lures of the world. Thank you for always being willing to take me back whenever I have chosen to stray from you! I alone am responsible for any distance between us: you *never* leave me. Jesus, use whatever it takes to keep me interested in reading the Bible, attuned to your voice, dedicated to prayer, and committed to love others as you love me."

by Lisa Cheater

Two faced ...

"The one who says he is in the Light and yet hates his brother is in the darkness." - **1 John 2:9**

It's easy to let your opinions slip out: "I can't stand that guy." "I totally hate her!" "I wish he would go die in a hole!" You may feel disappointed in someone or hurt by their actions, but because I love you always, even when you disappoint Me, you cannot let hate have a place in your mind. Christian love is a choice, *not* a feeling. Let go of your anger. When you feel the urge to blurt out malicious words, say "Jesus, save this person" instead.

Now what? *Pray:* "Jesus, it's so hard to let go of my hatred because I feel entitled to it! It makes me feel right! Still, I know this is not how you want me to behave. Right now, I admit to feeling extreme hatred towards _____(name person)_____. Nothing comes from loathing except high blood pressure, so remove the malice in my heart, and sweep my mind clear of any traces of anger. Place your hand of deliverance upon this individual, and bring him/her to a saving relationship with you."

233

Why'd you do that?

"For what I am doing, I do not understand; for I am not practicing what I would like to do, but I am doing the very thing I hate." - **Romans 7:15**

It's a startling thing, isn't it, to catch yourself doing something you know is wrong. You want to show love, then you find yourself despising someone. You want to be kind, then you pick a fight with your sibling. You want to be obedient, but sassing your mom is easier. This is the nature of being human. Your tendency to sin constantly fights against My teachings, like a daily boxing match. The only way to win is to surrender your attitude and actions to Me every day!

Now what? *Pray:* "God, I am not perfect, nor am I flawed. I am human. You have made me with a free will to choose my actions, attitude and behavior. And though that means I will make the wrong choices sometimes, it also means I get to be *ME*, not someone else. I am free to be exactly the person you created! You are amazing, Lord! Lay your personality on top of mine, that I may make the very best decisions for my life."

by Lisa Cheater

Ouch!!!

"Every branch in Me that does not bear fruit, He takes away; and every branch that bears fruit, He prunes it so that it may bear more fruit." - **John 15:2**

I see so much potential in you. You mistake My correction as punishment, but it's just the opposite! I allow a few hardships into your life to make you stronger as a Christian and bring you closer to Me. I am proud of you, your many talents, and I know you are able to be so much more than you are today. Rest in My plan and just see what we can accomplish!

Now what? *Pray:* "Lord, I know you only correct and prune those you love, but the process of shaping my will into your really hurts at times. I don't want to be snipped from the vine and discarded. I want to bear fruit, to do things that lead others to a relationship with you and expand your Kingdom here on earth. Thank you for loving me enough to care about the effectiveness of my life."

235

Deep in love . . .

"And He said to him, 'You shall love the LORD your God with all your heart, and with all your soul, and with all your mind.'" - **Matthew 22:37**

Sold-out love is the coolest. It's all-encompassing, all-consuming. It penetrates every thought and every action. You wake and sleep thinking of your true love and the things about them that make your heart flutter. You can't wait to talk and laugh together. That is the nature of loving God! Only the Father can guide your day, hold your hand when you're alone, and calm you down when you're afraid. Give our relationship all you've got! I did. I gave it My life.

Now what? *Pray:* "Jesus, come near to me today, right now! Because you make your home inside words of praise, I lift up your Holy name. You are my master, best friend, guide, shelter, constant companion, and unshakable best friend. Never in all of history has there been a pure and perfect life except for yours! Help me love you with all my heart, soul, and mind every day, for your love endures all things. Forever. Thank you, Lord!"

by Lisa Cheater

Finish what you start …

"Now finish the work, so that your eager willingness to do it may be matched by your completion of it, according to your means." - **2 Corinthians 8:11 (NIV)**

It's tempting to blow off responsibilities because you're tired or too busy, but it's so important to actually show up and do whatever you have promised. The process of getting to a goal is more important than the goal itself for it demonstrates your reliability and strong character. Instead of quitting, see your tasks as ways to worship Me with your time.

Now what? *Pray:* "Jesus, I have quit things in the past, and the feeling of giving up was horrible. Though the tasks ahead of me are long and difficult, give me the perseverance I need to finish. One task I am especially overwhelmed by is: _____(name it)_____. Lord, you never give up on me, so help me cross this finish line, with my best work, as a gift to you!"

... lights, and, action!

"This is My commandment, that you love one another, just as I have loved you." - **John 15:12**

Obedience isn't based on emotion. I love you no matter what, and I expect you to love others no matter what. Don't look to *feel* the love. It will make you resentful. Instead, show love through behavior that is patient and kind, and your heart will likely follow. Sometimes it's better to *act* your way into a new way of feeling. Behave in a loving way and your feelings will change.

Now what? *Pray:* "Jesus, my world is filled with selfish messages like: 'be true to yourself and don't give in to anyone.' Movies and music pound this theme home. The world expects me to live for myself, yet I know these ideas directly conflict with your perfect way. Today, let me demonstrate love toward someone I may have looked down upon in the past, remembering this is the way you love me, unselfishly, and unconditionally."

by Lisa Cheater

Big pay off...

"While he was still speaking, a bright cloud overshadowed them, and behold, a voice out of the cloud said, 'This is My beloved Son, with whom I am well-pleased; listen to Him!'" - **Matthew 17:5**

People who gathered to see Me die also saw the power of My Father on that day. All My suffering, teaching, and journeying was worth it to hear My Father say, "Well done." I am more than a good person, historical figure, or a wise preacher. I am the Son of God who loves YOU and knows you by name! When you fully realize that, you will *want* to obey Me! Then I can say to you, "good job!"

Now what? *Pray:* "Lord, I long to hear you say, *'well done'* to me. I want my life to make you smile. Every day I'm on this earth I have the chance to be your hands, feet, and mouth, so let my actions serve as proof of your amazing love. Reveal your plans for my life through open and closed doors of opportunity, and as I encounter challenges today, may I be careful to respond as you would."

239

There is always a way out ...

"No temptation has seized you except what is common to man. And God is faithful; He will not let you be tempted beyond what you can bear. But when you are tempted, He will also provide a way out so that you can stand up under it." - **1 Corinthians 10:13 (NIV)**

I never allow you to be tempted beyond what you can handle with My help. Some burdens may seem too heavy for you, because they are! If you never had to deal with things beyond your abilities, you wouldn't need Me! I can give you the strength and resources to make it. Talk to Me. Listen to My Word. Your faith grows stronger each time you move through, and past, your temptations.

Now what? *Pray:* "Thank you, Jesus, for this reassurance. I know that you teach me to resist temptation through opportunities to resist it, not by some giant wave of your hand. Just knowing that you never allow me to face a temptation greater than I can handle is a promise that fills my soul with relief and courage. I do not *have* to give in when my friends try to pressure me to do something I know is wrong. Though the exit may not always be clear, I will look for it now in every tempting situation."

by Lisa Cheater

Big words...

"Always giving thanks for all things in the name of our Lord Jesus Christ to God, even the Father;" - **Ephesians 5:20**

There are two humongous words in this scripture: *always* and *all*. Don't pick and choose for which things to be thankful. I ask you to be grateful for everything at all times. That's really hard to do, I know, but here's why: thankfulness pushes out fear, hate, and jealousy, the things that eat you away inside and make your life miserable. Gratitude leaves you feeling blessed and whole. Stop and offer thanks right now for something in your life.

Now what? *Pray:* "Lord, I often take my blessings for granted, but I do thank you for ____(name something you're grateful for)_____! Uttering a thank-you for good things is easy, but being grateful for *all* things, including hard times, is not. So, I will also offer you this sacrifice of gratitude, giving thanks though I may not feel like it, for something in my life that is a challenge, like: _____ (name it)_____. I know you are working through this situation to sharpen my faith because you love me so much and know what's best. Thank you, Jesus."

241

Speed dial to Heaven ...

"Listen to my prayer, O God, do not ignore my plea; hear me and answer me. My thoughts trouble me and I am distraught." - **Psalms 55:1-2 (NIV)**

Those cell phones can dial up a pal in no time at all. Two buttons, one scroll, or a simple voice-command...it's pretty impressive. Believe it or not, calling Me is faster than the best 4G network on the planet. As quick as you can breathe in enough air to say the word, "God," I'm there. You have a direct line to Me, no waiting, no dead zones, no fees, no breaking up, no busy signal. Wouldn't AT&T like to be on My network? ;-)

Now what? *Pray:* "Jesus, there are few worse things than calling up my friends when I desperately need to talk, and going straight to voicemail. I feel let-down, alone, and deserted. But you are *never* too busy to take care of me or listen to my cries for help! With you, I am never alone no matter where I am, or how limited the cell service. You pick up before I even breathe your name! Come and envelope me with your presence today, Lord. Thank you!"

by Lisa Cheater

Do-overs rock!

"Therefore we have been buried with Him through baptism into death, so that as Christ was raised from the dead through the glory of the Father, so we too might walk in newness of life." - **Romans 6:4**

I am the Lord of second chances! The moment you believe in Me and call on My name as your Savior, you get a new life, a new path to walk that leads to Heaven and contentment on earth. Even though I won't instantly free you from all negative consequences of your choices, when you choose Me over the world it's like I've brought you back from the dead - the numbness of sin. So, choose to smile today, for you and I have a bright future ahead.

Now what? *Pray:* "Jesus, I am so thankful for your grace because I mess up every single day. My human nature shows up in my temper, my words, my temptations, my attitude, and negative habits. Though I share this struggle with every other Christian on the face of the planet, I ask you to help me be more like you. Today, empty me of myself, and fill me with your voice, your attitude, and your kindness."

243

Responsible to lead others . . .

"Anyone who breaks one of the least of these commandments and teaches others to do the same will be called least in the kingdom of Heaven, but whoever practices and teaches these commands will be called great in the kingdom of Heaven." - **Matthew 5:19 (NIV)**

Your influence over others is stronger than you think. People watch you, wondering what guides your life and how you make decisions. Whenever you can, encourage your friends to stay on the right path. Don't let them lead you astray. Instead, lead them to make sound decisions and behave in a way that pleases Me.

Now what? *Pray:* "Jesus, I never really thought about how easily I encourage others to sin. When I jibe my pals to post mean comments or videos on the internet, or add to their anger and gossip, I am leading them astray. You've called me to be a peacemaker! Give me wise words to speak to my friends when they need encouragement and gentle correction."

by Lisa Cheater

Picture of Heaven . . .

"He will wipe away every tear from their eyes; and there will no longer be any death; there will no longer be any mourning, or crying, or pain; the first things have passed away." - **Revelation 21:4**

It's hard to imagine any world without sadness, pain, evil or corruption, but that's exactly the place I've prepared for you. The Christians you have known who have passed away, family members and friends, are already enjoying this awesome Heaven where they're not sick and no one cries! Hearts don't break here! You'll get to see them again someday, but for now don't worry about them or wonder where they are. They're with Me and cheering you on!

Now what? *Pray:* "Lord, the image I have of a cheering section in Heaven, just for me, fills my heart with joy! I miss my Christian family and friends, but I know they are in a perfect place without any worries or pain. I long to see them again someday, but until then, help me make today and every day count for your Kingdom."

Know when NOT to speak ...

"Do not give what is holy to dogs, and do not throw your pearls before swine, or they will trample them under their feet, and turn and tear you to pieces." - **Matthew 7:6**

To a pig, a gemstone is just one more rock on the ground; it'll never understand or appreciate a diamond's value. Some people have hearts so hard toward Me, they can't relate to you at all. Christianity is a foreign concept because they do not have the Holy Spirit in their hearts, and they may laugh or make fun of you no matter what you say or how sincere your words. Pray for them, then let them be. Focus your time with friends who build you up as a Believer and with those who are genuinely ready to know more about Me.

Now what? *Pray:* "Lord, help me understand that I do not have the ability to make people change their minds about you. My task is to pray for the lost, answer their questions (or find someone who can), and to live a life above reproach so others will desire to have a relationship with you."

by Lisa Cheater

He said, she said . . .

"Keep a clear conscience, so that those who speak maliciously against your good behavior in Christ may be ashamed of their slander." - **1 Peter 3:16**

Who has said something mean against you? Was it true, honestly? When people hurl nasty, untrue rumors about you, *they* look like the fool. On the other hand, make sure you don't give anyone a reason to talk badly about you. As you learn more about My character, you'll become more like Me, and you'll know with certainty when your behavior needs checking.

Now what? *Pray:* "Jesus, look through my life and see if there is anything displeasing about the way I live, the choices I make, my attitude, and the words I use each day. Forgive me if I am at fault, and give me courage to apologize to anyone I've wronged. Keep me so closely tied to you that I cannot slip, and make me immune to the hurtful lies of other people."

Tasmanian devils . . .

"He who is slow to anger is better than the mighty, and he who rules his spirit, than he who captures a city." - **Proverbs 16:32**

Just like the cartoon, real Tasmanian devils are crazy-wild Australian marsupials akin to a dog or a badger. They are always on the move, quick to take down prey with razor-sharp teeth. Sound like anyone you know? Maybe yourself at times? People with angry hearts act just like those Tasmanian devils, but to no gain. I bless the one who quietly thinks before acting out in a rage. Self-control, not brutish strength, is a trait of the mighty.

> Now what? *Pray:* "Jesus, teach me to be mighty in self-control, using your Word as my guide. Help me remember this scripture when watching movies, media, and video games that portray strength through giant weapons and a lack of self-control. Though the world would encourage me to do otherwise, enable me to hold my tongue and my temper when I'm angry."

by Lisa Cheater

248

The one rule ...

"Love does no wrong to a neighbor; therefore love is the fulfillment of the law." - **Romans 13:10**

Before I came to live on earth, people worried about keeping all of God's laws, the Ten Commandments. They made extra rules to punish people who broke the Commandments, but what they were missing was love. It's awesome to memorize all Ten Commandments, but if you just remember to love others and Me, you'll have the bases covered.

Now what? *Pray:* "Lord, today help me remember to love others and please you in all I do. I can never earn my way into Heaven by being 'good enough', and I am thankful for your grace and mercy that make it possible for me to be forgiven. Guard my mouth today so my words will be like beautiful music to your ears."

Be wary of wolves . . .

"See to it that no one takes you captive through philosophy and empty deception, according to the tradition of men, according to the elementary principles of the world, rather than according to Christ."- **Colossians 2:8**

For thousands of years, beautiful people from all different cultures and races have created man-made religions as an alternative to Me. Don't let yourself be drawn into another culture's ideas about God. You are not simple-minded for believing in Me as the one true path to Heaven. You are wise to acknowledge that I *am* the only way, and one day, all the world will know it, too.

Now what? *Pray:* "Jesus, I study world cultures as part of my academic education, but protect me from being lured into temptation by other religions and sects. They are not 'better' ways to Heaven. You are the only way. May the information I learn about these other faiths serve to deepen my desire for these peoples to come to know the real, one, Truth: You."

by Lisa Cheater

My agenda . . .

"So do not worry about tomorrow; for tomorrow will care for itself. Each day has enough trouble of its own." - **Matthew 6:34**

You have so much to do, so much to plan. I am so proud of you for being aware of your current responsibilities and for your courage to take on new tasks as you become a young adult. Prepare and organize your schedule, but avoid worrying about the future. Your fear of what *might* happen leaves very little room for Me to work. Take care of the things that must be dealt with immediately, but don't let your fear of tomorrow ruin today.

Now what? *Pray:* "Jesus, help me focus on today's most pressing tasks and avoid worrying over things that may or may not happen in the future. I know you hold every aspect of my life in your strong hands. Prevent my mind from drifting to anxious thoughts, especially over things for which I have zero control. Today is a gift from you. I will rejoice in it!"

Accusations 101 . . .

"Brothers, if someone is caught in a sin, you who are spiritual should restore him gently. But watch yourself, or you also may be tempted." - **Galatians 6:1 (NIV)**

"Accusations" is not one of the books of the Bible! Yes, as a Believer, it's your responsibility to help another Christian when they mess up, but do so with love and with gentleness. Confront your friend with truth and encouragement, not ridicule or blame. If your life has been a good example of righteous living, your friend will appreciate your concern.

Now what? *Pray:* "Jesus, grant me objective wisdom so that my words don't move ahead of your timing. Give me the right things to say to my Christian friends who seem to be struggling so they will feel lifted up rather than offended. Thank you for the opportunity to be a blessing to others and for dear friends who encourage me."

by Lisa Cheater

LOL...

"God has made laughter for me; everyone who hears will laugh with me." - **Genesis 21:6**

I'm no prude. I enjoy seeing you happy to the point of laughter, and I love laughing with you when you are surprised by an unexpected blessing. When it's not hurtful or aimed at another person's fumbles, laughter is the perfect response to creativity. Look carefully for all the humorous happenings I place in your path each day to cheer you up!

Now what? *Pray:* "Lord, this world is full of imagination and amazing creativity, but I'm usually so busy I fail to notice all your masterful handiworks: people, animals, landscapes, the universe. One part of creation that always makes me smile is _____(name it)_____. May this be a reminder that you are interested in even the smallest details of my life and plant many blessings along my path every morning. Don't let me miss them today!"

253

Remember, and forgive . . .

"A new commandment I give to you, that you love one another, even as I have loved you, that you also love one another." - **John 13:34**

September 11 is a difficult day to speak of loving others. Hatred and fear left their marks on the United States in 2001 and ignited movements of extremism all over the world. It is a sacrifice for you to love those that commit crimes against innocent people, but that's the very thing that should set Christians apart from the rest of the world. Be fueled by love, not hate. Let your love be visible, every day, as a witness to My goodness.

Now what? *Pray:* "Lord, only you can bring good out of 9/11. Be present in the lives of every family who lost a loved one on that day or any day marked by the evil deeds of terrorists. And though my human mind cries out for justice to be served against religious militants who murder innocent people, I pray you will help them see how they are wrong. May they turn to you for salvation. Protect our military, our country, and our people."

by Lisa Cheater

My force is with you ...

"For he has rescued us from the dominion of darkness and brought us into the kingdom of the Son he loves, in whom we have redemption, the forgiveness of sins." - **Colossians 1:13-14 (NIV)**

As you walk through your day, imagine that you are surrounded by a giant force field of light, My light. It's like a bubble that surrounds you wherever you go today. You can see through it, to the destructive things others say and do, but you are protected from the effects of darkness and hurtful words. Ask every day for My presence and protection. I am your shelter!

Now what? *Pray:* "Jesus, I can think of so many movies with this theme, where the good guys are rescued from some sinister lair and delivered to the safety of a righteous kingdom. That is exactly what you have done for me! I am no longer bound by the enemy. I am a member of your Holy family of adopted children! Keep that protective bubble around me tightly today wherever I go."

255

The power of love ...

"Above all, keep fervent in your love for one another, because love covers a multitude of sins." - **1 Peter 4:8**

Just how powerful is love? What keeps friends together through bitter arguments? What keeps a marriage together when communication breaks down? What makes you cry at the loss of a pet? What allows a parent to forgive disobedience and do twenty loads of laundry in a week? What would prompt a father to sacrifice his son for the sins of billions of people? Love. It's *that* strong.

Now what? *Pray:* "Jesus, thank you for your unending love. You paid with your life so that I would have a way into Heaven, then sent back a counselor, the Holy Spirit, to guide my thoughts and actions day by day. You are always here by my side, never absent, never too busy to listen. When relationships in my life go south, encourage me to love—above all else—just as you love me."

by Lisa Cheater

256

Avoid gossip . . .

"You shall not bear false witness against your neighbor." -
Exodus 20:16

How much of what you say each day is *about* someone else's
faults, problems, or mistakes? It's fun to make people laugh, to be
popular and feel listened to, but when you talk about one of My children
behind their back you're actually breaking one of My commandments.
Bearing false witness means more than lying. It means gossiping about
others as well. Do you want people slandering you? Dare to be different.
Speak the truth always.

> Now what? *Pray:* "Jesus, forgive me for gossiping
> about people, especially other Christians. In our sinful
> world, gossip is often a way to bond with other people,
> a common ground I have with others. I realize now how
> backward-thinking that is! Catch me when I'm about
> to say something unsubstantiated or hurtful behind
> someone's back. Let my reputation be built upon my
> truthfulness, dependability, and honesty."

Relationships 101 ...

"Then the LORD God said, 'It is not good for the man to be alone; I will make him a helper suitable for him.'" - **Genesis 2:18**

I created a design for successful relationships, and, as always, there are reasons for the plan. Women are different, but no less important, than men. Both are created by Me for specific skills and purposes. In general, women are more nurturing, intuitive, and good listeners. Men are usually problem solvers, strong, and driven. This isn't being sexist; these traits are not flaws, they are gifts that complement each other. Together in a balanced marriage under My leadership, a man and woman can create the basis for a strong family. Think about that when you start dating to discover My best for you.

Now what? *Pray:* "Father, thank you for the incredible way you've designed marriage! I don't have to apologize for the way you created me. I'm exactly the person you designed for a special relationship someday. Strengthen my respect towards the opposite sex, and give me confidence in your plan so my standards for a loving relationship will remain high."

by Lisa Cheater

258

I'm here . . .

"Indeed, the very hairs of your head are all numbered. Do not fear; you are more valuable than many sparrows." - **Luke 12:7**

I see every burden you carry and every challenge you face. Though you cannot physically see Me, I have not left you without help. My Word and My teachers are your counsel! Stop drawing your self-worth from what others say and think about you. You are My totally-loved child, My delight. I have chosen you to be a part of the Kingdom of God, and I will never leave your side!

Now what? *Pray:* "Jesus, thank you for loving me so unconditionally. I never have to pretend to be someone else with you. You see all of me: the good *and* the not-so-good parts in progress. Help me value your opinion of me above all others. Though I may try and fail at many tasks and activities in this life, I will always be perfect and wonderful in your eyes."

My address . . .

"Blessed are the pure in heart, for they shall see God." - **Matthew 5:8**

You won't find Me locked inside a church or hidden away in an altar somewhere. Nor will you find Me in the dark or amidst confusion and anger. I am located in the hearts of those who are at peace with My will and take the time to communicate with Me. Quiet your busy schedule for just a few minutes today. Sit and talk to Me. Use that still, focused time to renew your courage and release your stress.

Now what? *Pray:* "Lord, I long to be 'pure in heart,' with nothing negative between us. I admit that I am not always comfortable with your plans for me. In fact, I harbor resentment against you about: _____(name it)_____. Oh, Lord, help me see that your closed doors protect me from destructive situations! Help me acknowledge your sovereignty in every situation, especially when I don't get what I want."

by Lisa Cheater

The meaning of life . . .

"For we are His workmanship, created in Christ Jesus for good works, which God prepared beforehand so that we would walk in them." - **Ephesians 2:10**

Why are you here? It's a big question that lots of super-smart people have spent years trying to answer! The answer is really quite simple: you are here to experience God's love, to worship, and to share Me with others. You are My Father's masterpiece, a work of art, beautiful, strong, and creative. Never look down on yourself or another person, for you are insulting God when you condemn His design.

Now what? *Pray:* "Lord, I may not have been born to be rich and famous, but my birth was no cosmic accident. I have a purpose. My life is important. You knew all about me before I was conceived and have given me very specific gifts and abilities. Help me use those skills to glorify you every day. Thank you for all you've made me to be."

Shipped ...

"Therefore I say to you, all things for which you pray and ask, believe that you have received them, and they will be granted you."- **Mark 11:24**

Imagine a giant warehouse full of all the things you desire *according to My will* (note: this does not include a boatload of cash, unlimited shoes, and a date with a superstar). Things like faith, joy, wisdom, self-control, improved family relationships, a Christian friend, academic excellence, etc..., are stored in here. When you pray for something you KNOW I'd want you to have, I ship it immediately! You may not know the exact delivery date, but rest assured it's on its way to you. What do you need today?

> Now what? *Pray:* "Lord, you are not some fantasy godfather who gives me everything I ask for. You love me too much to give me things that would hurt me! Thank you for your promise to provide whatever I ask for within your will. First, help me learn more about what your will is for my life as I try to become more like you. Second, I ask for: _____(name it)_____, something I honestly believe you want for me. I long for your blessings, Lord. Thank you!"

by Lisa Cheater

I speak your language . . .

"In the same way the Spirit also helps our weakness; for we do not know how to pray as we should, but the Spirit Himself intercedes for us with groanings too deep for words." - **Romans 8:26**

Sometimes problems weigh so heavy, words can't even express your sorrow. You long to pray to Me, but you don't know where to start because the mess is so big. Other times, you don't even know what to pray *for*, you just know you need My help. Don't worry about the right words. Even if all you can do is cry, My Spirit hears the words of your heart, and I will answer. Coming to Me is all I ask.

Now what? *Pray:* "Jesus, the word *groaning* describes exactly how my soul feels sometimes! I don't have to come up with beautiful and catchy prayers for you to understand the language of my broken heart. In those times, when thoughts and sentences just won't come together because I'm in such deep despair, help me recall this scripture as a reminder that you always understand what I'm going through."

Don't give up . . .

"For God is not unjust so as to forget your work and the love which you have shown toward His name..." - **Hebrews 6:10**

I know My way is not easy for you. It's hard to reign in your emotions and actions when you feel like exploding, especially when you think you're right. Each one of your small spiritual victories is seen by My Father. Your Christian journey and discipleship (the process of becoming more like Me), is unique to you, and blessings abound for your determination to stay the course. Don't give up on yourself. I haven't.

> Now what? *Pray:* "Jesus, help me never lose my desire
> to be like you. Becoming like you takes time. Please help
> me be patient with the process. Destroy thoughts of self-
> doubt and guilt that creep into my mind when I fall. You
> are always here to lift me up and set me on the right path
> again. As you forgive me, give me strength to forgive
> myself."

by Lisa Cheater

'Nuff excuses!

"The LORD said to [Moses], 'Who has made man's mouth? Or who makes him mute or deaf, or seeing or blind? Is it not I, the LORD? Now then go, and I, even I, will be with your mouth, and teach you what you are to say.'" - **Exodus 4:11-12**

Many opportunities are out there for you to use the gifts I've given you. So why are you afraid? When you know I've called you to do something, rest assured I will give you the tools you need to get it done! I created your mind and your voice, and I'll never send you into a situation where you are certain to fail. You might think you're in over your head, but that discomfort leaves room for you to rely more on Me. In those times, call on Me for strength, trust Me, then do your best.

Now what? *Pray:* "Jesus, teach me to know the difference between *being sent* and *demanding to go*. I want to succeed in the tasks you want me to accomplish! When I insist on doing things my way and hope you'll follow along, I am doomed to certain failure. Be patient with me as I learn this lesson, and grant me fearlessness to step into unfamiliar situations for you."

Two way mirror . . .

"'For My thoughts are not your thoughts, Nor are your ways My ways,'
declares the LORD." - **Isaiah 55:8**

There are many situations in life that make no sense, and it's tempting to look up toward Heaven and say, "What the heck are you doing up there? I SO do NOT get your plan!" That's because My view of you is like a two-way mirror. I see all there is about you, every word, every fear. But you do not have the mind of God. It's impossible for you understand what I'm thinking, how I work, or why things happen, so don't spin your wheels trying to make human sense of a divine plan. Just rest in the knowledge that I am in control.

> Now what? *Pray:* "Lord, I do not understand your ways nor how you are working in my life, but I know someday it will all make sense, every trial, every joy, every challenge, every accomplishment. Until that day, I trust you with everything I am and will not question your work. Thank you, Jesus, for designing a meaningful life for me."

by Lisa Cheater

Guard your tongue . . .

"So also, the tongue is a small thing, but what enormous damage it can do. A tiny spark can set a great forest on fire." - **James 3:5**

You sometimes feel your words are justified because you're angry, but I know you regret them. Just as a small cigarette ash can start an entire forest fire, one spiteful word can launch a huge fight with others. Wise, calm words, however, can stop an argument in its tracks, just like dousing that fire with water. Remember that others are trying to see Me in you, and they are always watching. Commit to keep your tongue in check today, and let your words be helpful, not hurtful.

Now what? *Pray:* "Jesus, you are my perfect example of strength under control. I can feel the exact moment when my anger is about to boil beyond my ability to restrain it, and yet, too often I allow it to burst forth like a flame. Forgive me, Lord, for my carelessness. As I move through my day, help me keep my attitude, reactions, and words in check."

267

Friendship scale . . .

"A friend loves at all times, and a brother is born for adversity." -
Proverbs 17:17

On a scale of 1 to 5, what kind of friend are you (5 is super solid, 1 is a major deadbeat)? A loyal friend is always there to help in times of trouble and never says hurtful things to you or about you behind your back. And not only that, siblings are supposed to stick up for each other as well. Can you say that about yourself? Friends, brothers, and sisters are My gifts to you to help you through a really tough world. Make sure you are a "5" to them, too!

Now what? *Pray:* "Jesus thank you for the solid friends you have given me. They are like support beams that hold me up, and I am so grateful for them. Help me to weed out those who are inconsistent, deceitful, and mean-spirited, and may I be a true and reliable friend back to my siblings and friends."

by Lisa Cheater

No one will ever know . . .

"...be sure your sin will find you out." - **Numbers 32:23**

Every person has a secret or two, hidden sins that no one can see. Except Me. Although you are my beloved child, and I give you many opportunities to turn yourself around, people who do wrong always, *always,* get caught eventually. The enemy may let you think you're getting away with something for a while, but there will be retribution at some point. Don't test that fact. Stay close to Me and there will be nothing to hide!

Now what? *Pray:* "Lord, thank you for perfect justice that is reliable and righteous. Make me a clean vessel with nothing to hide, no secrets to unearth. I can't hide anything from you, God. Help me remember this verse when I am angry over someone who seems to 'beat the system' with their evil ways. You see all of us, the kind and the cruel, and will pay back deeds in your own time."

269

Sow the seeds . . .

"Therefore, my beloved brethren, be steadfast, immovable, always abounding in the work of the Lord, knowing that your toil is not in vain in the Lord." - **1 Corinthians 15:58**

You may never actually see many of the results of your work as a Believer, but you never know how or when the seeds you plant will sprout. People you've talked to about Me may become a Christian years later, or kindness you show today may inspire someone to begin a ministry tomorrow. Don't be discouraged if you feel like you aren't making stuff happen for the Kingdom. You are! Every day you live for Me is important!

Now what? *Pray:* "Jesus, thank you for reminding me of my value. Though my pride often makes me feel disappointed when I don't see tangible results of my Christian walk, I know now that you are using me, my noble moments *and* my failings, together for good. I cannot see everything you're accomplishing though me, but I know you are doing amazing things."

by Lisa Cheater

Prayer when you're sad . . .

"Why are you in despair, O my soul? And why have you become disturbed within me? Hope in God, for I shall again praise Him for the help of His presence." - **Psalms 42:5**

Sometimes your soul needs a little wake-up call. Your heart is heavy and you forget to concentrate on the power of My Father to handle ALL situations— large and small. Pray this verse today and remind yourself that the Creator of the Universe is sitting right next to you, ready to help you through this tough time and restore your hope.

Now what? *Pray:* "Thank you, Lord, for giving me the option to choose hope. I have no reason to walk around sad and moody like people who don't know you and truly have no hope! My faith is in you, God, and I praise your Holy name for your mighty hand that helps me in all situations. Restore my attitude to one of joy today."

Down time ...

"In the early morning, while it was still dark, Jesus got up, left the house, and went away to a secluded place, and was praying there." - **Mark 1:35**

My ministry to do the Father's will was the most important thing in My life on earth, yet it didn't consume My every waking hour. Even I would have burned out without taking frequent time-outs alone to pray and talk to God. I loved the early hours when everything was still and silent. Pray first thing in the morning, before your feet touch the floor, for the strength and wisdom you'll need to handle the day's problems.

Now what? *Pray:* "Jesus, just as I need to put on a coat before I leave the house in winter, I need to surround myself with your presence first thing in the morning to prepare my attitude for the day. Help me remember to ask for your protection and wisdom as my first order of business when I wake up. Give me courage to face the world clothed in joy."

by Lisa Cheater

Christian pressure?

"Finally, be strong in the Lord and in the strength of His might." -
Ephesians 6:10

An acorn doesn't become an oak tree overnight. Growth takes time and nourishment. In the same way, don't expect to be a perfect Christian immediately or become overwhelmed by all the things you are learning like scripture, confession, prayer, loving grumpy people... You don't have to understand it all at one time! Today, just concentrate on two things: loving Me and loving others. If you can do that, the rest will eventually fall into place as an extension of your devotion.

Now what? *Pray:* "Lord, I do love you and am so thankful for the lessons of truth that you bring me each day. Today, I will encounter all kinds of people. Some will be easy to like; others will be hurting and harboring a negative attitude against the world and everyone in it. Help me love them unconditionally, with kindness, soft words, a calm spirit, and a smile."

273

Instant gratification?

"Wait for the LORD; Be strong and let your heart take courage; Yes, wait for the LORD." - **Psalm 27:14**

You live in a world of instant feedback. Lightning-fast technology makes it possible for you to get an answer on any question almost immediately. It's easy to get used to that way of thinking. Sometimes My guidance and direction is quick, and sometimes it seems slow in coming. In those times, I ask something very difficult of you: wait patiently on Me. I answer every prayer in My time and always in a way that is best for you. Be encouraged, even if you must wait a bit.

Now what? *Pray:* "Jesus, forgive me for pulling the reigns from your hands and trying to steer my life the way I want. I am not God. You are. When I push to make things happen, it usually falls apart. Give me patience to wait without complaining for your answers, on your time schedule. I will rejoice in however you choose to answer my prayers, Jesus, for I know it will be your best for me."

by Lisa Cheater

Team sport . . .

"But keep on the alert at all times, praying that you may have strength."-
Luke 21:36

Professional soccer is exhilarating to watch. Every player's
position is structured to work together in order to advance the ball to
the goal. Each team member must pay attention to the game and the
location of other players in order to win. Your Christian friends and
leaders are part of your spiritual team! You are not expected to reach
your goals alone. Access the strength of other Believers who are there
to help you.

Now what? *Pray:* "Lord, I am so grateful for the
Christian men and women who are part of my spiritual
team. They are your hands and feet and voice here on
this earth! Specifically, I thank you for this leader in my
life: ____(name Christian)____, and ask you to bless
them for their willingness to serve and encourage me.
Equip me to someday be a guiding light for another new
Believer, too."

Fill up here . . .

"But the Lord is faithful, and He will strengthen and protect you from the evil one." - **2 Thessalonians 3:3**

You have many things vying for your attention each day, and it is critical that you take some quiet time to pray and read My word. That time is sacred; it keeps you plugged into My will, My direction, and My peace. As you pray back to Me in a moment, I will give you the strength and confidence you need to stand firm in an unpredictable world.

Now what? *Pray:* "Lord, your Word says you are as close as my breath, so let me let me take time to breathe deeply today, and in doing so, invite your Holy Spirit to be present in my day. Block out all the distractions that keep me from focusing on your voice, and speak clearly to my mind so I cannot possibly miss your direction! Thank you, Jesus, for being the only pure and perfect remedy for my stress. I love you."

by Lisa Cheater

I paid the tab . . .

"Now all these things are from God, who reconciled us to Himself through Christ and gave us the ministry of reconciliation." - **2 Corinthians 5:18**

Imagine taking ten of your closest friends to the nicest restaurant in town. You have a blast all evening, then comes the bill. You dig through your wallet and find you have zero cash and no credit card. You owe the restaurant a steep debt! Then along comes some guy you've never met who pays the whole tab. His only request is that you help others as he helped you. THAT is reconciliation! It's what I did for you on the cross when I paid your debt of sin with My life.

Now what? *Pray:* "Jesus, thank you for dying on the cross so that I can receive grace and eternal life with you! Because of your sacrifice, I can share a deeper understanding of love with other people. That's the ministry of reconciliation. My friends and I aren't doomed to live sad lives in desperate situations. We have you as our deliverer! Grant me boldness to share that good news with someone today."

Don't worry!!

"Look at the birds of the air, that they do not sow, nor reap nor gather into barns, and yet your Heavenly Father feeds them. Are you not worth much more than they?" - **Matthew 6:26**

I know where every critter on earth hides. I am aware of all they need to eat and where they should sleep. I see when a sparrow falls from the sky and when a new rabbit is born. Animals are very trusting. They never fret about what they need. I provide it in abundance. That's the way I take care of you when you rely on Me. Ask for what you need, not just things you *want*, and I will provide.

Now what? *Pray:* "Lord, place within me a grateful heart that never worries about the necessities of living. Teach me to trust you with all aspects of my life, especially as I move beyond high school and college and into the real world. Show me how to plan without being anxious, how to save without being greedy, and to be thankful for everything I have."

by Lisa Cheater

I am your defense...

"Contend, O LORD, with those who contend with me; fight against those who fight against me." - **Psalms 35:1 (NIV)**

I am your defense against any opponent who challenges your faith and your character. It's tempting to want revenge upon those who hurt you, but you must let Me deal with them and resist the urge to "set 'em straight." Call upon Me with this prayer, not in a demand for justice, but with a sincere heart that seeks to be delivered from the wrongs of others. I am your helper, your army, and your fortress!

Now what? *Pray:* Jesus, you are my contender, my challenger, against my enemies. Why do I spend so much time feeling beat down by people, especially those who are not Christians and don't know any better? Rise up against those who hate me, and protect my heart from hurt and despair, Lord. I will place my faith in your goodness, fairness, and justice."

Perfection not a prerequisite . . .

"Therefore repent and return, so that your sins may be wiped away, in order that times of refreshing may come from the presence of the Lord;"- **Acts 3:19**

No one is perfect, not the best-behaved person you know, not even your parents. Christianity isn't about being good, it's about becoming. The more you seek after My ways, the more like Me you'll become. Where you are struggling? Tell Me where you have fallen. Crawl out from under that blanket of self-pity and guilt, and restore Me as the Lord of your life.

Now what? *Pray:* "Lord, sometimes I feel so far away from you I don't think I can't possibly find my way back. But I know you are never too far to hear my cries for help. Bring me back into your arms of love and acceptance. Forgive me for tossing you on a shelf and letting you sit there for days on end while I live my life my way. Please, Lord, return to your place as my leader, my guide, my captain."

by Lisa Cheater

You ARE worthy!

"If you then, being evil, know how to give good gifts to your children, how much more will your Father who is in Heaven give what is good to those who ask Him!" - **Matthew 7:11**

I am not a huge, mystical entity in the sky who doles out punishment and goodies on a whim. That's so far from the truth! Even the most mediocre dad on earth knows what his children need and takes care of them, so, then, don't you think My Father in Heaven knows every single thing you need and desire? He loves to send special blessings to His children. Just don't forget to ask!

Now what? *Pray:* "Father, people, even parents, let us down all the time, but you are always reliable, always here, and always loving. You are the perfect dad. The proof is in stories of how you've led and guided your children over the millennia, even when they were disobedient. You know what I need most. Bless me in some special way today, Lord."

Good girl, good boy ...

"If we say that we have no sin, we are deceiving ourselves and the truth is not in us." - **1 John 1:8**

Life Situuquation #6: Honesty + Repentance = Forgiveness

Now what? *Pray:* "Who am I trying to convince, Lord, when I take pride in my own goodness? You already see my faults, and I cannot experience a guilt-free life without confessing them to you and asking for help in conquering them! Forgive me for my feelings of superiority and conceit! I am not perfect, and I daily wrestle with: _____ (name it)_____. Teach me to overcome my weaknesses."

by Lisa Cheater

One God . . .

"You alone are the LORD. You have made the Heavens, the Heaven of Heavens with all their host, the earth and all that is on it, the seas and all that is in them. You give life to all of them and the Heavenly host bows down before You." - **Nehemiah 9:6**

Some cultures and religious practices may seem interesting, but don't let your mind become confused by their teachings: I AM the only way to Heaven. I AM the only Creator, the only Savior, the only way to God the Father. Study My Word for Truth, and pray this scripture from the prophet Nehemiah as a shield against all the contradictory religious theories you may encounter.

Now what? *Pray:* "Lord, protect me from the multitude of media and celebrity testimonials that tout the latest and greatest spiritual movement. They are worthless! Let me recognize Truth instantly, remembering that YOU alone are Lord, creator, life-giver, and King of all nations."

283

Enough already!

"The Lord is not slow about His promise, as some count slowness, but is patient toward you, not wishing for any to perish but for all to come to repentance." - **2 Peter 3:9**

One day I WILL come back to earth, and when I do, Satan and everything he stands for will be gone forever. Evil will be blitzed and only joy and peace will remain! Sounds awesome, right?! So why not end all the suffering and come back now? Because there are still so many people who have not heard about Me. I am waiting for as many people as possible to become My followers before I return so that they will have a chance for eternal life. Think about your pals today. Who needs to hear about me? Will you tell them?

Now what? *Pray:* "Jesus, you are so good and patient. I never realized you may be waiting for someone in my circle of friends to accept you and that I may be the key. One person you bring to my mind who needs you is: _____(name them)_____. I pray the circumstances in his/her life will take them on a journey that leads to you. Should our paths cross, give me the courage and right words to tell this person about your awesome gift of salvation."

by Lisa Cheater

Cure for the blahs . . .

"Then our mouth was filled with laughter and our tongue with joyful shouting; Then they said among the nations, "The LORD has done great things for them." - **Psalms 126:2**

Today may seem unremarkable to you. Maybe you are tired of the same old routine day after day, or wish something extraordinary would happen, like winning the lottery or seeing your favorite celebrity in person. Well, cheer up because today IS special! You are alive and loved by Me! Right now, think of three things that you are thankful for, and I promise your day will seem instantly brighter.

Now what? *Pray:* "Jesus, I need your energy today to fight fatigue and boredom. I don't have the strength to make it through this day, but you do. In this time when life may not seem all that spectacular, I will focus on the blessings you've given me, like: _____(name three things)_____. You have done great things for me! Thank you, Lord, for them all."

285

I am your Warrior ...

"'Then afterwards,' declares the LORD, 'I will give over Zedekiah king of Judah and his servants ... into the hand of Nebuchadnezzar king of Babylon.'" - **Jeremiah 21:7**

Throughout history I have stood beside My people and allowed them to conquer nations, enemies, and territories in My name. I exalt those who are champions of doing right! I am formidable in any battle, so trust Me with that burden you are carrying on your shoulders! Your job is to do your best, stay focused on My will, and give Me the challenge of righting wrongs and carrying out justice.

Now what? *Pray:* Lord, thank you for being my gracious helper and bold warrior! I do not have to fight all my battles alone; you actually *want* me to hand them over to you! Lord, I lay all my burdens at your feet now and leave the outcomes to you. Keep my attention focused on doing the right things ."

by Lisa Cheater

Where to focus . . .

"Now accept the one who is weak in faith, but not for the purpose of passing judgment on his opinions." - **Romans 14:1**

Maybe that buddy at church plays hurtful pranks on you, or your Christian friend at school has a foul mouth. Maybe they don't know as much about Me or the Bible as you do, but that doesn't give you the authority to think yourself superior to them. Like you, they still have much to learn about being a Believer. Their growth as a Christian is just that: THEIRS. Concern yourself with your own behavior, and leave judgment to Me.

Now what? *Pray:* "Jesus, help me to see my Christian friends with your eyes. Just like me, they are imperfect, learning, and becoming like you however you find best to teach them. I do not have to be a doormat for anyone, but I am not responsible for anyone else's actions or behavior. Only mine. Today, give me a merciful spirit, and keep me focused on *my* walk with you."

Better than Wikipedia . . .

"But if any of you lacks wisdom, let him ask of God, who gives to all generously and without reproach, and it will be given to him." - **James 1:5**

I am the God of wisdom and direction. Don't let your mind fret about how to handle a situation! You are learning more and more about what behaviors line up with My will, but you can also ask Me to help you learn in school. I will give you peace to focus, knowledge to organize your notes and thoughts, and the discipline to study. Ask Me. My direction is tried and true, and always reliable.

Now what? *Pray:* "Lord, each year it seems that school—life—gets more and more complex. The challenges increase, the work gets harder, I get more stressed. Bring peace and clarity to my thinking so I can do my best in school. Sharpen my ability to discern right from wrong with wisdom and courage. Make me an honorable witness before my friends and a light that points them to you."

by Lisa Cheater

I'll never give up on you . . .

"For I am confident of this very thing, that He who began a good work in you will perfect it until the day of Christ Jesus." - **Philippians 1:6**

You are My chosen disciple, and I have a wonderful design for your life. Because I understand your potential, I will never give up on your out of frustration. Don't be discouraged if you feel you aren't making progress as a Christian. I began working in you the day you accepted Me and won't stop until we meet in person.

Now what? *Pray:* "Jesus, thank you for never giving up on me. I am so grateful that you are a God of second, third (and usually more) chances, and you stand ready to pick me up when I fall. I understand that I'm a spectacular work in progress, and a new layer is woven into the tapestry of my life each day. You are making something wonderful of my life, and I can't wait to see what you have in store for me."

In over your head?

"I am God, the God of your father; do not be afraid to go down to Egypt, for I will make you a great nation there." - **Genesis 46:3**

You have many things in your life you wish you could avoid. Situations force you to step out on faith, and it can be intimidating. Take courage! Throughout history, I have sent many people like Moses, Joshua, David, Esther, and Paul to do unthinkable tasks - things they felt completely unable and unequipped to do at first. Whatever I call you to do, I will enable you to do! Don't be afraid! Put your trust in Me and My word. I will take care of you.

Now what? *Pray:* "Lord, help me today to face my assignments unafraid. From schoolwork to mission work, give me the confidence I need to complete the things you have asked of me. You will never let me down, no matter how hard the task. Don't let my fear of failure prevent me from completing what you've called me to do. I trust you, Lord."

by Lisa Cheater

Bigger than bad ...

"... greater is He who is in you than he who is in the world." - **1 John 4:4**

I am greater, mightier, and more powerful than anything evil in this world. Thieves, gangs, bullies, liars, murderers are no match for Me. The Holy Spirit that lives inside your heart and speaks to you about right and wrong, is capable of breaking down any evil stronghold. Let it loose by living like Me! your gentleness obliterates hatred. Your joy dissolves depression. Speaking the truth exposes darkness. You are my mightiest weapon!

> Now what? *Pray:* "Lord, sharpen my faith so I can be a strong and effective sword in your battle against evil. Make my life a clear example of your mercy, love, and power. Keep my thoughts and actions pure, my words in line with your will, and my attitude attuned to yours. Let me stand as a testimony to your greatness so that all may know what an awesome God you are!"

291

The party has to end ...

"There is a time to give birth and a time to die; A time to plant and a time to uproot what is planted. A time to weep and a time to laugh; A time to mourn and a time to dance." - **Ecclesiastes 3:2,4**

Everyone loves the joy of springtime, but without winter there would be no spring. Seeds must die in order to be reborn as a new plant. Just as every season has a purpose, every season of your life has a purpose. When you allow your sinful nature to die by repenting and accepting Me as your Savior, you become like that seed - ready to be sown, watered, and grown into a new life as a Believer. Life has ups and downs, but sad times help you enjoy the happy times even more. If you are in a sad season right now, rejoice, for it will soon give way to a time of joy.

Now what? *Pray:* "Lord, I will not let myself become bogged down in misery. You have promised a new day of joy! If things were always good I would never learn to depend on your power! Lord, help me trust you during times of sadness. Strengthen me so I can help others who are struggling, too."

by Lisa Cheater

Perfect escape ...

"Yet those who wait for the LORD will gain new strength; They will mount up with wings like eagles, They will run and not get tired, They will walk and not become weary." - **Isaiah 40:31**

I know you are tired and frustrated. The harder you try to work towards your goals, the further behind you feel. Don't be discouraged by setbacks. Come hang out with Me, read in the Bible about how I handled tough problems and people, and I will renew your ability to keep going. Just when you think you can't go on one more day under all the pressure, fall into My arms, and I will be the wind in your sails.

Now what? *Pray:* "Lord, the wind in my sails right now feels more like a hurricane, and I'm hanging on for dear life. Clear my mind of distractions and worry that paralyze me from taking action. Set my day according to your plan and priorities so I don't become bogged down by unnecessary tasks. Calm the winds of anxiety, and replenish my strength so I can sail smoothly today with you at the helm."

293

Sunday closeness . . .

"But the Lord is faithful, and He will strengthen and protect you from the evil one." - **2 Thessalonians 3:3**

Just as texting while driving can distract you from the road and lead you into a serious accident, taking your eyes off Me can cause you to fall into temptation. Even so, the sly schemes of the enemy are no match for My power. Remember the things you learn in Bible studies and from your parents and church leadership. Don't leave My teachings at home or confine them to Sundays. Take Me with you wherever you go this week.

Now what? *Pray:* "Lord, sometimes it seems my memory is wiped clean as soon as I leave church on Sunday morning. I experience you in worship, I am touched by scripture that is read, then it all fades like blowing sand once I'm back in the real world. Today, help me recall the verses and teachings I have learned. Bring scriptures to my mind that address the issues I face so I can experience 'Sunday closeness' every day of this week."

by Lisa Cheater

294

Inside out . . .

"And do not be conformed to this world, but be transformed by the renewing of your mind, so that you may prove what the will of God is, that which is good and acceptable and perfect." - **Romans 12:2**

Focus your thoughts on My ways, and don't let yourself become distracted by all the sin around you. What are "My ways"? Everything you learn from the Bible about me: My attitude, My teachings, My goals, and My behavior. It's not enough just to act nice around others. As My true follower, align your mind, your thoughts, with Me every single day. Be *in* the world, but not *like* the world.

Now what? *Pray:* "Jesus, may my commitment to live like you be evident in my life, both in public and in private. May the world see a life that is positive, joyful, strong, and reliable, and may you see a heart that is imperfect but willing, hopeful, honest and pure. Help me keep my promises to you even when the world wants me to behave in the opposite way. Thank you for loving me with abundance and daily renewing my courage with your goodness and mercy."

295

I am for everyone...

"...to them He gave the right to become children of God, even to those who believe in His name..." - **John 1:12**

I did not suffer and die on the cross for Americans only, or for only Jews, white people, the rich, the popular, or any other race. I came so ALL people from ALL nations could be saved! Anyone, of any race, from any country, who believes in Me and calls on My name is My beloved! See others today as I see them, and speak to them as I would. Never forget that you are My audible voice on earth!

Now what? *Pray:* "Jesus, forgive me for looking upon others as inferior, for judging them and considering myself better than they. Today, let me see people with a different set of eyes. As I observe those who are poor, spiritually or financially, help me remember that you love them just as much as me. Embolden my character that I may speak words of hope or offer a smile to anyone who needs it."

by Lisa Cheater

296

Evil starts here …

"For the love of money is a root of all sorts of evil, and some by longing for it have wandered away from the faith and pierced themselves with many griefs." - **1 Timothy 6:10**

Money itself isn't a bad thing. It buys food for the needy and helps pay the bills of your home and church. Loving money above Me, however, is a terrible thing. Greed causes people to do whatever it takes to get more cash, even at the expense and loss of others. How do you avoid loving money? Keep Me first in your life. Be grateful for whatever you and your family *does* have, avoid jealousy, and save up for things you can't afford to purchase right now.

Now what? *Pray:* "Lord, you are more precious than any amount of money and more desirable than any pile of gemstones! Your love for me lasts forever! I am grateful for the material things with which you have blessed me. When envy sneaks into my thoughts, replace it with gratitude. Help me be a good steward of the money you allow me to have, careful to give back to you, to save, and to spend carefully."

Fresh miracles daily . . .

"Great are the works of the LORD; they are studied by all who delight in them." - **Psalms 111:2**

It's cool to imagine a whole sea parting in the middle and columns of fire descending from Heaven to stop bad guys in the nick of time. I did those things! Even so, people on earth are so complex and cynical that most believe the miracles they witness each day are mere coincidence. Today, look for miracles, large and small, in healings and in mercies, in My creation of nature, and in random acts of kindness. You'll see I'm still in the miracle business.

Now what? *Pray:* "Jesus, the depth of your love and grace for us is amazing! Your hands made the earth and your voice spoke life into existence! How awesome is that? Don't let me miss a single miracle today! Make me aware of each and every special gift and incredible wonder you float through my life. Thank you for these gifts of encouragement. They remind me you are near and watching me all the time, holding me close in the palm of your hand."

by Lisa Cheater

Today, reprogram your heart . . .

"...let us strip off every weight that slows us down, especially the sin that so easily hinders our progress." - **Hebrews 12:1**

When computers begin to run slow and internet surfing bogs down, it's usually time to clean some unnecessary and harmful software off the hard drive. Once the drive is straightened up, a computer can run as it was originally designed. Likewise, I created you to be free of worry, fear, anger, malice, jealousy and gossip. That's all crud that weighs down your spirit and your witness. Uninstall that junk today, right now, and your heart will hum.

Now what? *Pray:* "Jesus, purge my heart of all the unnecessary negative junk that I've let accumulate. Feelings of self-hate, bitterness, pride, envy, laziness, blame, and hatred I place in the trash can of my heart and empty it before you, right now. Place a holy firewall around me so those things can never find a way in again. Thank you for your forgiveness!"

299

Ultimate shield . . .

"If God is for us, who is against us?" - **Romans 8:31**

Do not let your heart be bothered by the words and deeds of hateful people. Yes, words can be damaging, but I am so much more powerful than anything evil, including death itself! I am in your corner as My beloved. I've got your back! With Me as your best friend, don't worry about any enemy you come up against. Nothing can penetrate my My power and protection that wraps all the way around you like a metal armor!

Now what? *Pray:* "Jesus, why do I spend any time at all stewing over the mean deeds of others? Since you are for me, no one can stand up against me. Not because I'm great, but because your Word promises that you will go ahead of me, stand beside me, and guard behind me though every journey. So, then, I will not devote any more minutes to self pity and blame. I am a sheltered child of The Mighty King!"

by Lisa Cheater

Day 300

Planned history ...

"So all the generations from Abraham to David are fourteen generations; from David to the deportation to Babylon, fourteen generations; and from the deportation to Babylon to the Messiah, fourteen generations."
- Matthew 1:17

All of time, past and future, is clear to Me. That's a really hard thing to get your head around, but understand that everything in history has had a purpose and is part of a grander plan. Thousands of years before I was born, it was prophesied that I would be from King David's family. And I was. My death and resurrection happened just as predicted, too. I have a plan for your life, and all the things you are learning and going through now are preparing you to accept a special blessing in the future. You are not yet that person. Rely on Me to help you each day as you grow in faith and knowledge.

Now what? *Pray:* "Jesus, give me patience and strength to let you work in my life, developing my faith in the way you see fit. I know I have much to learn, and my selfishness makes it hard to wait for the perfect blessings you are designing for me. History proves you are a man of your word. I will trust you, Jesus, to lay out my steps in the best way."

Your safety net...

"...the Lord knows how to rescue the godly from temptation, and to keep the unrighteous under punishment for the day of judgment..."-
2 Peter 2:9

I am like a narrow bridge that safely takes you above and over a gushing waterfall. My path is not easy, but it is the very best, and will always protect you. Many people choose not to take that bridge; they would rather see if they are strong enough to swim over that waterfall. Don't test yourself with situations that might tempt you to sin. Cling to my bridge of safety, and keep away from places and things that will cause you to stumble.

Now what? *Pray:* "Lord, the calls for my attention are so hard to resist at times. Some days they sound like, *'what if...'* or *'no one will know...'* and *'everyone else is doing it...'* Lord, I need your wisdom to avoid temptation. I mostly struggle with ____(name it)____ right now. When sin tries to lure me in, keep me locked onto your strength and goodness to resist."

by Lisa Cheater

Who is your best friend?

"Two are better than one because they have a good return for their labor. For if either of them falls, the one will lift up his companion." - **Ecclesiastes 4:9-10**

Is your best friend someone who talks you into doing things you know are wrong, or is it a Christian who helps and encourages you to do good? Nothing is more important in your young life than a Believing friend. I designed friendship so you would have a physical pal to support you and help you be your very best. Make a pact with your Christian friend to always support each other.

Now what? *Pray:* "Jesus, thank you for my Christian leaders and friends, especially:____(name person)____. This person is always reliable and truthful, even when I don't want to hear it! Remind me today to take time to thank this friend for his/her impact on my life and to encourage others today."

Keep keeping on!

"Let us not lose heart in doing good, for in due time we will reap if we do not grow weary." - **Galatians 6:9**

Remember those races in PE? You got half way through the course and thought, "Oh boy, I'm gonna fall over right here." But you kept going and eventually finished the race. Sometimes it feels like you're getting nowhere by doing the right things; evil people just seem to keep getting ahead! I promise, there are rewards for staying strong. Of course, you will have a place in Heaven, but your stamina and determination encourage many others to follow Me right now. Don't stop living right, especially when life gets hard!

> Now what? *Pray:* "Lord, life is so hard sometimes, I do feel like giving up and crawling under a rock. But you see everything. Nothing gets past you. Grow my faith and shield me against discouragement. Give me a double helping of strength today so my faith will not falter."

by Lisa Cheater

304

Let's get 'er done . . .

"And looking at them Jesus said to them, 'With people this is impossible, but with God all things are possible.'" - **Matthew 19:26**

The problem before you is not too hard for Me. Your heart sinks when you think of the size of the task you wrestle with, and how hard it will be to complete it. But I can do anything, and so can you, with My help. Whatever I have called you to do in My will, you will be able to do. It may not be easy and it might take a while, but it's never impossible. Take one day, one step at a time, and we will get there. Together.

Now what? *Pray:* "Lord, with a single word you brought the universe into being. With a word you calmed the sea for the disciples. With a word you withered a fig tree. With a word you can lift the weight of all my problems and guide me through. Hear me, Lord. Today, help me organize my tasks and accomplish the impossible with your help."

Holy GPS...

"Trust in the LORD with all your heart and do not lean on your own understanding. In all your ways acknowledge Him, and He will make your paths straight." - **Proverbs 3:5-6**

Your life is full of choices and decisions, and every day brings a new set of challenges. "Which way is correct? What is the right decision? What should I do?" Pray for guidance in all those decisions. I never meant for you to do these things alone! Life is an open book test, and the open book is the Bible. Remember the Truths in My word, and listen to the direction of your parents, teachers, and authorities. That's how I communicate with you about which way to turn.

Now what? *Pray:* "Though many things don't make sense to me, Jesus, I trust you. I will not spin my wheels trying to figure out why things happen or what someone else is thinking. I give you my life, my dreams, my plans, and my path. Wherever you lead, I'll go. Whatever you call me to do, I'll do. Make your will very clear to me. Guide me through opportunities, and close doors that might take me down wrong paths."

by Lisa Cheater

Don't fret, be happy ...

"In this you greatly rejoice, even though now for a little while, if necessary, you have been distressed by various trials." - **1 Peter 1:6**

What's to rejoice about when you're distressed by trials? Here's four things: 1) As My child, you are promised a reward in Heaven, 2) Your faith is strengthened most during hard times, 3) The commitment you demonstrate during trials encourages others to believe in Me, and 4) Choosing to be joyful when things aren't going well makes you feel better! It's impossible to be sad and grateful at the same time, so rejoice in good times and in bad!

Now what? *Pray:* Jesus, I know my difficulties will pass in time, some sooner than others, so hold me true to my faith as a Christian as I push through the most challenging obstacles. Peter knew a great reward awaited him in Heaven for his dedication to you. Give me that kind of sold-out enthusiasm and perseverance to keep doing the right things. Let me see problems as chances for me to learn something fabulously new about your character. And mine."

307

Don't wait for Thanksgiving ...

"Give thanks to the LORD, for he is good; his love endures forever." -
Psalms 118:1 (NIV)

I am with you every day of every year. My love and goodness
never end, although there are times you think I've gone on an
extended vacation and left you to fend for yourself. Not so! Look
around you and be thankful today for the many blessings I've given
to you. The very fact that you can read this is one! Do you have a
bed? That's another! When you take time to thank Me, you'll be
reminded of how much I do for you.

Now what? *Pray:* "Lord, I take so many things for
granted. You have blessed me with so much. Forgive me
for complaining and whining about how hard my life is.
Three specific things I am thankful for are ____(name
them)____. You are always good and always merciful,
Lord. Thank you for sharing your abundance with me.
Teach me to use everything I have to honor your name."

by Lisa Cheater

Love covers . . .

"God is love, and the one who abides in love abides in God, and God abides in him." - **1 John 4:16**

It's not possible to really love others without Me. You *want* to be loving and kind, but the harsh words and cruel deeds of others make it so hard. Those hurts roll around in your head at night as your replay the scene over and over. Let all those hurts drip off you like water. Imagine Me covering you with a warmed blanket. That's what it feels like to abide in My love. Now take that feeling with you to school, to work, to practice, wherever you go.

Now what? *Pray:* "Lord, conceal me within your blanket of perfect love. Calm my drifting thoughts and angry attitude so that the evil words and deeds of others bounce off me like arrows against a rock. Today, let your love shine through me in thoughtful speech, purity, respectfulness, and kindness."

All you need . . .

"The LORD is my shepherd, I shall not want." - **Psalms 23:1**

Shepherds take their jobs very seriously. They would never lead their flock into danger or to an area without adequate food. The sheep don't complain or try to analyze the shepherd's chosen path; they simply follow, knowing their guide will take them to a safe pasture. That is how I want you to be with Me. Stop resisting My direction, and simply rest in the flow of my blessings. I will take care of you!

Now what? *Pray:* "Jesus, you are my careful and loving shepherd. I will follow where you lead me, even if the way seems unclear or hard. I will not question or argue your ways, Lord. I know you only take me to safe pastures of great blessing, so help me to trust you today as you guide my activities and steer me through all kinds of situations."

by Lisa Cheater

Gift source . . .

"Every good thing given and every perfect gift is from above, coming down from the Father of lights, with whom there is no variation or shifting shadow." - **James 1:17**

Although I sometimes allow difficulties to help you learn and develop stronger faith, trouble does *not* originate in Heaven. I am the Father of Light, the very opposite of darkness. Every good and positive thing in your life came from Me, and My intent is always to shower you with blessings!

Now what? *Pray:* "Father, thank you for brightening my day with perfect gifts. You are always reliable, for unlike the stars and sun whose light flickers and casts moving shadows throughout the day, your goodness never changes and never wanes. Help me shine like a bright star set against a world of darkness."

Scootch over ...

"Abide in Me, and I in you. As the branch cannot bear fruit of itself unless it abides in the vine, so neither can you unless you abide in Me."-
John 15:4

Nearly every small child will, at some point, tell her parents, "I can do it by myself!" That's a cool thing about growing up. You're learning to be self-sufficient, but don't become so independent that you don't *want* to need anyone, especially Me. When you fill up yourself with selfish pride you don't leave any room for Me to help, and you will wither like a branch cut from a vine. Stay connected to Me, your vine to the Father, so I can sustain you at all times.

Now what? *Pray:* "Jesus, I know I am unable to bear fruit, to make anything good happen for your kingdom, without your help. Anything I am, all that I've accomplished, I've done so because you allowed me to. Remove my stubborn pridefulness. Thank you for reminding me that you are my source of creativity, skill, insight, determination, and strength. I know I am capable of many neat things, but only if I remain a part of your vine."

by Lisa Cheater

Money 101 ...

"'Bring the whole tithe into the storehouse, so that there may be food in My house, and test Me now in this,' says the LORD of hosts, 'if I will not open for you the windows of Heaven and pour out for you a blessing until it overflows.'" - **Malachi 3:10**

Tithing means giving at least 10% of the money you make, and it's requested of every Believer, regardless of age. I know it's hard for you to save cash, (there are so many things you want to spend it on!), but I want you to trust Me with everything, including your money. Try this: of all the money you make in a month, give 10% to your church, save 10%, and you can spend the remaining 80%. Just wait and see how I will bless you for your faithfulness! If you learn to manage your money like this now, you will avoid serious debt in the future.

Now what? *Pray:* "Jesus, I admit that money is important to me, just as it was to people of your day. I don't want the pursuit of wealth and riches to become a god to me, though, now or in the future. Give me the discipline to give back to you what is yours by tithing, to save a portion of what I earn, and to make wise decisions about how I spend the rest. May I be a generous giver and use the money you've entrusted to me to help others."

Jesus freak ...

"See how great a love the Father has bestowed on us, that we would be called children of God; and such we are. For this reason the world does not know us, because it did not know Him." - **1 John 3:1**

Don't be upset when people think you're nuts for believing in Me or call you names because they can't understand why you won't join in along with them. You are blessed for standing up for righteousness! Those who do not get Me will not get you. Until the Holy Spirit reaches into their heart and gives them a clue, don't expect the spiritually blind to see.

Now what? *Pray:* "Lord, protect my heart against feelings of despair and hurt when my non-Christian friends or acquaintances belittle my faith. I cannot expect them to act like Christians if they're not! I ask that you touch my pals who are lost. Create in them a desire to seek you and learn what it means to have a real relationship with a loving God! I will not take their stubbornness personally for only you can change their minds."

by Lisa Cheater

No small god . . .

"Who does great and unsearchable things, wonders without number?"-
Job 5:9

Today, right this very moment in time, I am listening to you, working through a soldier in Afghanistan, caring for a child in India, healing a woman in Switzerland, bringing rain to a town in Australia, and helping a teenager in Sudan find hope. Not to mention the millions of other people, events, miracles and star births I am in the midst of! I'm busy, yet I know your full name, the moment you were born, every fear that keeps you up at night, and how many hairs are upon your head. Never doubt the breadth of My strength and My love!

Now what? *Pray:* "You are amazing, Jesus. I get so wrapped up in my own little world where I am the center of the universe that I forget the zillions of needs that you handle each and every day, every hour! Your incredible omnipotence is more than my human mind can fathom! You hold our whole cosmos together yet still have plenty of time to hear my daily problems and worries. Thank you, Lord, for your ability to be everywhere at once."

Power source . . .

"But in all these things we overwhelmingly conquer through Him who loved us." - **Romans 8:37**

The Marvel comic book character, Iron Man, requires a bizarre energy device in his chest in order to stay alive. If this power source is removed or runs low on juice, he loses strength, but with it (and a cool metal suit), Iron Man is a formidable hero. I am *your* power source! I can't promise superhuman powers, but to My followers, I promise the ability to conquer every foe you encounter with Truth. Keep Me in your heart at all times for uncommon courage!

> Now what? *Pray:* "Jesus, help me remember this verse whenever I face a giant obstacle. You are always with me, inside my heart, and I can overcome anything. Your word can stand up against any person, evil, temptation, problem, worry, and challenge. I am a conqueror because of your love!"

by Lisa Cheater

Procrastination is disobedience?

"So Joshua said to the people of Israel, 'How long are you going to wait before you go in and take the land that the LORD, the God of your ancestors, has given you?'" - **Joshua 18:3**

The Israelites put off dividing up the land of Canaan because no one wanted to do it. It was a boring, tedious process, but it needed to be done in order to organize the tribes. When you put off assignments, chores, responsibilities and other tasks that are expected of you, it prevents you from moving forward and shows a lack of respect for authority and God. Manage your time by prioritizing the day's activities well.

Now what? *Pray:* "Jesus, forgive me for putting off tasks that I simply don't enjoy or don't want to do because they're so enormous. As I encounter the temptation to procrastinate today, help me remember that my laziness might cause me to miss out on some future blessing! What things do I have to get done today? ____(name them)____. Develop in me the habit of using my time wisely as a way of showing my appreciation for all you do for me."

Time to reset . . .

"Restore to me the joy of your salvation, and sustain me with a willing spirit." - **Psalms 51:12**

Feeling pressed, distressed, and unrest? You can reset your attitude and your focus by memorizing this scripture. Say it to Me, as a prayer, and mean it with all your heart. Restoring hope and strength is My specialty, dear child! Commit these words to memory, and say them whenever you feel beaten down by the world. I will come to your rescue.

Now what? *Pray:* "Lord, the author of my hope in Heaven, restore me to the joy of your salvation, and sustain me with a willing spirit. Though I am tired and worn out by the pressures of this world, you are my renewing strength. Bring me back to the way it felt when I first accepted you as my Savior. Thank you, Jesus."

by Lisa Cheater

318

Let it rain . . .

"Therefore everyone who hears these words of mine and acts on them, may be compared to a wise man who built his house on the rock." - **Matthew 7:24**

Hurricane-force winds can rip down virtually any structure, but it's often the tidal surge that causes the most damage. Water quickly moves the shifting sand out from under homes close to the shore and the structures collapse. However, buildings constructed upon rock have no chance of going down because their foundation is sure. I am the solid foundation for your life. Anchored in Me, none of life's crazy storms can destroy you.

Now what? *Pray:* "Jesus, as I learn more about your teachings, help me integrate them into my life as a solid foundation for living. Your way guides me through what is right and wrong. It lifts me up with promises that keep me from becoming depressed, and it helps me make wise decisions for everything from dating to money. Let me never stray from you, Lord! Keep me on solid ground for all my days."

Living Word...

"The grass withers, the flower fades, but the Word of our God stands forever." - **Isaiah 40:8**

Of all the awesome stuff man has learned to make, he's never been able to come up with a living organism, plant or animal, that can last forever. Genetic experiments, clones, flower hybrids...they're cool, but they all have a shelf life. They will die. My Word has been around since before the earth was formed, before language existed to write it down, and will last to the end of time and beyond. It's not just a book, though, it IS alive because scripture has the ability to change how people think and feel.

Now what? *Pray:* "Lord, my parents and leaders often talk about 'the good old days' and how much easier life was in the past. Sometimes they say they can't believe how far away from you our culture has become. Their observance proves just how much public opinion and social tolerance has changed over time. Still, your ways are always right, never changing, never shifting. Help me to stand boldly according to scripture even when the rest of the world is wandering off in the wrong direction."

by Lisa Cheater

Passing through...

"For our citizenship is in Heaven, from which also we eagerly wait for a Savior, the Lord Jesus Christ;" - **Philippians 3:20**

There are many times when you feel as though you simply don't fit in – anywhere. I know that feeling, too. I had many followers, but I also angered lots of religious people. The world is hostile to Christians because you shine light on its many faults. But don't spend another moment depressed or disappointed about it. The world is not your permanent home. You have citizenship, already, in Heaven with me. Your ultimate residence is perfect, free of sin, and full of eternal joy.

Now what? *Pray:* "Jesus, it's hard to live as a Christian because so many of the people around me don't see the point. It's like I'm a visitor in another land, where the normal customs are different from my beliefs. I'm proud to be a citizen of Heaven, though, chosen by you for a tour-of-duty here in this world. Encourage me with your peace and Christian friends with whom I can share my struggles."

321

Beach church?

"Let us not give up meeting together, as some are in the habit of doing, but let us encourage one another." - **Hebrews 10:25 (NIV)**

It's tempting to sleep late on Sundays, claiming you're too tired to make it to church, but being with other Believers is really important to your growth as a Christian. It's a safe place where once a week you are surrounded with other people who love Me and face the same challenges at school or at home as you. Worship and prayer connect you *to* Me, and Bible study and fellowship enhance your knowledge of how to live *for* Me. Make church attendance a habit you can't live without!

Now what? *Pray:* "Lord, I gain so much strength from being with other Believers, especially those who are further along in their spiritual growth than me. If I have become lax in attending church, spur me to make the commitment each week. If I go but complain and grumble about it, fill my heart with gratitude. If my motive is just to meet cute girls/guys or enjoy the music, refocus my attention back on you."

by Lisa Cheater

Guard your sight . . .

"The eye is the lamp of your body; when your eye is clear, your whole body also is full of light; but when it is bad, your body also is full of darkness." - **Luke 11:34**

What's the first thing you are tempted to do when you are told to *not* look directly at a solar eclipse? To look at it! The temptation to sin feels just like that, so be careful what you allow yourself to observe. What you witness and hear becomes part of you, your personality, and it can influence your choices. Feeling uneasy at a movie, when texting, or at a party is the Holy Spirit directing you to get out of there! Protect yourself from temptation by guarding what comes in your eyes and ears.

Now what? *Pray:* "Jesus, I hear and see so much garbage each day, that I am sometimes immune to its effects. That's how comfortable I've become with it! Lord, give me the courage to say *no* to inappropriate music, movies, games, or language. Every day, help me stand up for what is right and avoid temptation."

323

Quick! In here!

"He who dwells in the shelter of the Most High will abide in the shadow of the Almighty. I will say to the LORD, 'My refuge and my fortress, my God, in whom I trust!'" - **Psalms 91:1-16**

In the movies, the hero always seems to find a hiding spot at just the right time, out of reach of the enemy. I am *your* hiding place, your immediate shelter. Whenever you feel threatened, angry, attacked, or powerless, come to Me in prayer instead of complaining or escaping with alcohol, drugs, video games, sex, or food. Pour out your fears to Me, and I will be your defense against all the troubles of the world.

Now what? *Pray:* "Lord, teach me to make decisions that keep me beneath the shelter of your wings. Never let me become so enamored by the world that I choose to move from under the safety of your shadow. I trust you, Lord, with my life and my future. Thank you for being my strong tower, the Most High God, the one safe place I can always run to in times of trouble."

by Lisa Cheater

Short memory ...

"As far as the east is from the west, so far has He removed our transgressions from us." - **Psalms 103:12**

I have forgotten all your past sins, so why do you keep bringing them up? Your genuine confession and repentance erases your mistakes. I don't hold sins over your head. The only one who can make you feel guilty is you. The next time Satan brings to memory a past failure for which you have already received forgiveness, remember this verse. In Me, you are free from persecution!

Now what? *Pray:* Jesus, thank you for your forgiveness and mercy meant for imperfect people like me. My past mistakes make me feel like a loser, a failure, and a total misfit. One mistake I have a really hard time letting go of, is: ____(name it)____. Lord, you have forgiven me for this. Take away the place I've created for it in my memory. May it never reenter my thoughts for you have forgotten all about it already."

325

Jesus who?

"Therefore everyone who confesses Me before men, I will also confess him before My Father who is in Heaven." - **Matthew 10:32**

You may not deny knowing Me like Peter did when he was questioned about being My disciple, but staying silent when a group of friends curse My name or hurt others, is the same thing. Maybe you don't want to offend them or make them think you are some religions nut for protesting against their inappropriate behavior. But if they are truly your friends they will respect your courage and loyalty to Me. Be brave. Speak up.

Now what? *Pray:* "Jesus, this is one of the hardest things in my life: speaking out against wrong at the risk of losing pals or popularity. But I cannot deny how much you have done for me! Give me the courage to stand up against evil, even if it means I may suffer ridicule by my friends in doing so. I will not take their jabs personally, for I know that to please you is far better than trying to please people."

by Lisa Cheater

I'm the author of your life . . .

"A man plans his course, but the LORD determines his steps." -
Proverbs 16:9 (NIV)

Your life is like a road that takes you around all kinds of towns, people, and situations. The journey can be tiring, and sometimes the right way is unclear. Shortcuts are enticing: maybe you'll just pray when you're in trouble, or create a plan you can control so you don't have to wait on My timing. The Bible details the way you should go and avoid falling off life's jagged cliffs. Let Me dictate your plans instead of asking My approval for things you've already decided to do.

Now what? *Pray:* "Jesus, prevent me from thinking I'm smarter than you! When planning or making choices about my life, may you be my *first* stop, not my last. I will consult you before I commit to activities, schools, jobs, and relationships. One big decision I have to make soon is: ____(name it)____. Guide me in this situation, Lord, according to your will."

327

Be grateful . . .

"You shall not covet your neighbor's house; you shall not covet your neighbor's wife or his male servant or his female servant or his ox or his donkey or anything that belongs to your neighbor." - **Exodus 20:17**

You may not be wishing you had a neighbor's donkey, but what about his Xbox, her iPhone®, her house, or their car? Wishing you had what someone else owns leads to discontent, jealousy, and sometimes, theft. Instead, look around at all the things I have given you. Stuff is just that – stuff. It can be stolen, lost, broken, and destroyed, but My love remains forever. Think of 5 things right now for which you are thankful, and your jealousy will dissolve.

Now what? *Pray:* "Lord, evil is often disguised as bright shiny things, material possessions that become idols and take my attention from you. Forgive me for wanting someone else's material blessings. Five things I'm thankful for are: ____(name them)____. You have entrusted these things to me and I am grateful! Thank you, Jesus, for all your good gifts."

by Lisa Cheater

Always mine . . .

"For I am convinced that neither death, nor life, nor angels, nor principalities, nor things present, nor things to come, nor powers, nor height, nor depth, nor any other created thing, will be able to separate us from the love of God, which is in Christ Jesus our Lord." - **Romans 8:34-39**

You will never lose your salvation. Once you become a Believer in My life, death and resurrection, and choose to follow Me, your place in Heaven and My help through the Holy Spirit are guaranteed, no matter how many mistakes you make. Salvation is not based on how good you are! Using guilt, the enemy may try to tell you otherwise, but I am always with you, ready to rescue and forgive. Stop beating yourself up for not being perfect. You are a beautiful work in progress.

Now what? *Pray:* "Jesus, I am so glad that my place in Heaven isn't dependent upon how perfect I am because I mess up on a daily basis. We all do. That's one thing that makes us human; we have the *choice* to do the right thing. Forgive me for my failures, Lord, and change my heart more and more each day to become a likeness of you. Thank you for your patience!"

329

Shed the old . . .

"Therefore if anyone is in Christ, he is a new creature; the old things passed away; behold, new things have come." - **2 Corinthians 5:17**

You've seen the process by which a lowly caterpillar transforms into a soaring butterfly. It's amazing! When you accept Me as your Savior, something similar happens. Your old "self", one without a desire to please Me, is shed, and you become new on the inside. You no longer need to hang on to old habits and behaviors. Don't try to put that old skin back on because it's comfy and familiar. Let go of the past, and learn to fly!

Now what? *Pray:* "Jesus, thank you for reminding me that I am not destined to be a ground-hugging caterpillar, a sinner condemned to a life of despair. I am a magnificent creature in your eyes because you are changing me from the inside out! Prevent me from hanging on to old sinful habits. Stay close to me so I won't be afraid to step out of my comfort zone and grow as a Believer."

by Lisa Cheater

Give it up . . .

"And Jesus, crying out with a loud voice, said, 'Father, INTO YOUR HANDS I COMMIT My SPIRIT.' Having said this, He breathed His last." - **Luke 23:46**

These were among My last words in ultimate surrender to My Father. It may sound like I was giving up, but I knew that mighty things would be accomplished because of My death. I knew I would return from the grave! What are you holding onto that you need to surrender to me? Tell Me. I will handle it for good.

Now what? *Pray:* "Jesus, some things are so hard to let go because they take away my control. Even though my plans usually lead to disaster, I still hang on to certain feelings and issues. Lord, as an act of faith, into your hands I commit this situation: _____(name it)_____ . You already know about it, the outcome, the best course of action. Lead me clearly, Lord, as I surrender my way to you."

Horn in . . .

"My God, my rock, in whom I take refuge, my shield and the horn of my salvation, my stronghold and my refuge..." - **2 Samuel 22:3**

Think about how animals use their horns. Sometimes horns are a weapon, sometimes they're used to gather food from trees. They are both a defense and a source of blessing. Likewise, I am your protector and your provider. So, why do you act as though you are without hope, without escape when you feel afraid, sad, lonely, despairing, stressed, angered, hurt, or depressed? I am your refuge!

Now what? *Pray:* "Father you are the horn of salvation and strength! You alone can guard me against my enemies and provide all the things that I need. Thank you, Lord, for standing with me though all life's twists and turns. Give me confidence today to face a crazy, struggling world. I can handle anything with you as my shelter, my ROCK!"

by Lisa Cheater

All in the attitude . . .

"Now Jabez called on the God of Israel, saying, 'Oh that You would bless me indeed and enlarge my border, and that Your hand might be with me, and that You would keep me from harm that it may not pain me!' And God granted him what he requested." - **1 Chronicles 4:10**

Jabez wasn't just asking for a bigger farm here. He was also asking My Father to bless him, his work, and to protect him from bad stuff. God approved his request because Jabez had the right attitude. Don't just ask to be a rock star. When you long for success, ask Me to protect you first because Satan loves to slide in on pride. Then ask Me to guide your decisions, bless your work, and expand your ability to reach others for Me. I'll do it!

Now what? *Pray:* "Jesus, I understand that being blessed by you doesn't necessarily mean being successful by the world's standards. It's not about being rich or famous, having lots of possessions or friends. It's about bringing as many people to you as possible using the gifts and talents with which you've blessed me. Expand my influence for you, Jesus. Use me however you see fit, and protect me from evil as I work to make your name known!"

333

Dying to self...

"I have been crucified with Christ; and it is no longer I who live, but Christ lives in me; and the life which I now live in the flesh I live by faith in the Son of God, who loved me and gave Himself up for me." - **Galatians 2:20**

When you die to your self, you allow My personality to lay over yours, not to completely replace your characteristics, but to fine-tune them. Every day, make it your focus to live for Me by remembering you are My hands when you comfort someone, you are My feet when you go someplace to help others, you are My voice when you encourage someone, and you're My face when you smile.

Now what? *Pray:* "Jesus, today give me the opportunity to let your character traits shine through mine. I can still be me, but with your temperament and love for others. Thank you for allowing each one of us to maintain our own special, unique identities while we develop Christ-like qualities. That's so cool! You have thought of everything! Place someone in my path who needs a glimpse of you."

by Lisa Cheater

334

S'all good ...

"My son, observe the commandment of your father and do not forsake the teaching of your mother; Bind them continually on your heart; Tie them around your neck. When you walk about, they will guide you; When you sleep, they will watch over you; and when you awake, they will talk to you." - **Proverbs 6:20-22**

What use are all these scriptures if you never think about them beyond the time they take to read? All of these words, all of these verses you've read, are full of supernatural power! They are reminders of what to do when you are angry or feeling confused, and that I am your first love when you are feeling down and alone. Keep these words in your heart at all times. Memorize them. They'll see you through everything in life.

Now what? *Pray:* "Jesus, thank you for the Bible, and all the wisdom in its words. Even when I am completely alone, you are able to speak to me by helping me recall verses that encourage, inspire, uplift, direct, and strengthen me. Show me which ones are my theme verses, the ones that most relate to my personality and needs, and enable me to remember the words so they are always with me."

You're worth it . . .

"Therefore when Jesus had received the sour wine, He said, 'It is finished!' and He bowed His head and gave up His spirit." - **John 19:30**

I could have avoided the cross. I could have called angels to rescue Me and destroy all those who persecuted Me. But I was led to die not to become some decorated martyr like many others in history, but for your sins. You are that valuable to Me. Your personality and gifts are aligned just so, in a combination that no one else has. Even now, you are learning to use those skills to bring hope into a lonely world. That's why I made the sacrifice. For you.

Now what? *Pray:* "Jesus, I may never fully comprehend the depth of your love and sacrifice for me, but I thank you for bridging the gap between sinful people and a Holy God. Thank you for loving me when it feels like no one else does. Thank you for dying and then rising from the grave so we can have confidence in your promises and your power. You alone are worthy of praise."

by Lisa Cheater

Still the same ...

"Jesus Christ is the same yesterday and today and forever." - **Hebrews 13:8**

Because your friends are human, just like you, they have the capacity to let you down. It's heartbreaking when someone who was your close pal last week suddenly turns on you or leaves you out of his or her plans this week. I am not like that. I'm the same man who taught in the synagogues over 2,000 years ago, and I love you and care about your disappointments today. Place your trust in Me. I'll never change on you.

Now what? *Pray:* "Jesus I can always count on you to be here when I need you. Your Word says that even before I speak your name to call for help, you begin answering my prayers. Scripture is a tangible reminder of your unfaltering, unchanging, unshifting, love for me. Even though I am changing every year, growing in maturity and knowledge, you remain my steadfast rock, the strong shoulder always available to carry me though anything."

337

True or false?

"Salvation is found in no one else, for there is no other name under Heaven given to men by which we must be saved." - **Acts 4:12 (NIV)**

Here's a T-F quiz for you: Allah, Baal, Buddha, Tao, Confucius, Dali Lama, Hari Krishna, and Yahweh are all names of God? FALSE! There's only one: Yahweh. He is the God of Israel, of Abraham, and of David, Creator of the Universe, God the Son, the Holy Spirit, Jesus. No other name leads to the assurance Heaven and joy on earth. My holy name declares Me as Savior. Trust no other gods or people who try to confuse you with false religions and teachings. Rest assured in your faith. I *am* the way.

> Now what? *Pray:* "Lord, God, only your name is to be exalted above all others. Help me be open-minded when learning about other cultures but never sidetracked by the claims of their religions, for of all these various beliefs, only Christianity is based upon a Savior that rose from the dead! I will place my faith and life in your hands. You are the real deal, Jesus!"

by Lisa Cheater

Life's answer key ...

"I am the door; if anyone enters through Me, he will be saved, and will go in and out and find pasture." - **John 10:9**

There are very few things in life that are 100% guaranteed, but here's one: you will be disappointed if you expect things or other people to bring you happiness. Popularity, the right clothes, the perfect boyfriend/girlfriend, a nice car, the sweetest phone on the market, a high from drugs or alcohol - they're all temporary. The peace I provide through prayer and by living out my teachings is the only perfect, good-for-you escape.

Now what? *Pray:* "Jesus, may I never attempt to find solace in other people, stuff, or substances. Yes, we all have a hole in our hearts that longs for acceptance, comfort, love, and assurance, but that hole is God-shaped. Only you can fill it. Only you can perfectly provide all the things my heart cries out for! Thank you, Lord, for accepting me as I am!"

339

Let go, let Jesus ...

"When I am afraid, I will put my trust in You." - **Psalms 56:3**

How much do you really trust me? Will you give a situation to Me when it seems hopeless? Will you cry to Me instead of sinking into denial or complaining to your best friend? Will you step back and calm yourself during an argument and let Me intervene? Try Me! I am capable of all you need and more. I can do the unthinkable and the impossible. Today, give Me every circumstance, every issue, every need.

Now what? *Pray:* "Lord, when I'm in a crisis, teach me the habit of coming to you in prayer, just as I would my best pal. You are closer to me than any person on this earth, so I can say anything to you, even my most heart-felt disappointments and fears. The most amazing thing is that you can actually do something about my problems! You can give me courage, remove obstacles, change someone's heart, or point me in a different direction. Though friends can offer support, help me trust you, first, in any situation."

by Lisa Cheater

Praise for gloom?

"This is the day which the LORD has made; let us rejoice and be glad in it." - **Psalms 118:24**

It's easy to praise My name when the sun is shining, you're at the beach, and you just found the perfect chair beneath a perfect palm tree. But when it's cold, rainy, and you're overwhelmed with homework, chores, commitments, and relationships - not so much. I love it when you praise Me with joy during those icky days because I know it's so hard for you; it's a sacrifice. When you praise Me when you don't feel like it, I bless you with incredible peace that comes from obedience.

Now what? *Pray:* "Lord, on those days when it feels like nothing is going right, whisper a reminder for me to stop and praise you. I don't have to feel happy, I just need to remember that even in the midst of the worst trials, you have a plan, a design, for good in my life. I know I have a Savior who loves me unconditionally, and that's one thing for which I am eternally grateful, Jesus. Help me be glad today."

DAUI is wrong . . .

"And do not get drunk with wine, for that is dissipation, but be filled with the Spirit." - **Ephesians 5:18**

Driving while drunk is certainly against the law, but I say that *Doing Anything Under the Influence* of drugs or alcohol is wrong. First, your laws say drinking under the age of 21 is illegal (and you are called to obey your government officials). Second, substances can cause you to do things you normally would never do. Resist the temptation to go along with the crowd at some party. Live what you believe, and walk away. Strength of character is always attractive!

Now what? *Pray:* "Lord, whenever I am exposed to drugs or alcohol, let me remember your commands to simply leave it alone. One sip, pill, or puff has the potential to pull me down a fast-sliding slope of sin and destruction. Help me reexamine relationships with people who are involved in these things, and surround me with solid Christian pals who make it easier to avoid temptation. Protect me from this popular escape, Lord. You're all I need to feel better."

by Lisa Cheater

Guilty?

"...but sanctify Christ as Lord in your hearts, always being ready to make a defense to everyone who asks you to give an account for the hope that is in you, yet with gentleness and reverence." - **1 Peter 3:15**

Would you be convicted of being a Christian if you were put on trial for your faith? Would there be enough evidence in the way you live your life every day to prove your allegiance to Me, or would the prosecution see that you are only half-hearted in your belief? Think about it now, because someday someone will probably ask you about your choice to follow Me as your Savior. Make sure the evidence is there!

Now what? *Pray:* "Jesus, when I accepted you as my Savior, you chose me to be a light of hope to all the people that I come in contact with: friends, family, teachers, strangers. Does the way I live my life back up my claim to be a Christian? I want others to know my faith is real. Place in me boldness and courage to defend you and my confidence in your promises. May I never be ashamed to claim you as my Lord."

343

The 15 second self-exam . . .

"All the ways of a man are clean in his own sight, but the LORD weighs the motives." - **Proverbs 16:2**

The next time you have a big decision to make, ask yourself these two questions: 1) Is my attitude, my motive for doing this, pleasing to the Lord, and, 2) Will my actions harm my witness for Christ or strengthen it? You can't cheat on this. I know what's really in your heart. If your motives are full of malice or selfishness, you best bag your plans. But if you honestly desire to please Me or reach the lost, you will succeed. Let everything you do be for the Glory of God, My Father!

Now what? *Pray:* "Jesus, I rarely think of you when I forge down the path toward my own plans. Until I get into trouble. Forgive me for handling my life all backwards. What is it you want me to do? How can I please you today? Keep my motivations pure and honest as I develop the talents and skills you've given to me."

by Lisa Cheater

Lost and found ...

"In the same way, I tell you, there is joy in the presence of the angels of God over one sinner who repents." - **Luke 15:10**

Think about something valuable you temporarily misplaced. Remember the crazy feeling of doom, panic, and fear? You wanted to cry and scream like a little kid! The idea of it being lost forever was insane! Then, remember the relief when you found it? (or maybe your mom or dad found it for you) You were so relieved! THAT is how I feel over any person who prays to accept Me as their Savior, or for the one who returns to Me after drifting away for a time. Heaven holds a massive party for every single soul that chooses to follow Me.

Now what? *Pray:* "Jesus, I am filled with joy just knowing that you care so much about me, my life choices, and my victories. Thank you for placing physical supporters here in my life, and for creating a cheering squad just for me in Heaven! I can relate to that feeling of never wanting to let go of something precious to me, the same way you feel about me. Thank you for that kind of perfect love."

Two faced . . .

"No servant can serve two masters; for either he will hate the one and love the other, or else he will be devoted to one and despise the other. You cannot serve God and wealth. " - **Luke 16:13**

Have you ever gotten caught between two warring friends? If you try to help one, the other gets mad. It's a no-win situation with you caught square in the middle. In the same way, you cannot serve God and live a lifestyle that is driven by a desire for money or possessions. You will become caught in the midst of two very different demands for your time, your resources, your thoughts, and your attitude. If you choose God, make sure to keep all other pursuits in proper perspective.

Now what? *Pray:* "Lord, do I love anything else more than you? Reveal to my heart where I have placed technology, stuff, money, clothes, or gadgets before you. I know the obsession with wealth leads only to disappointment and heartbreaking stress. Reset my priorities if necessary so that serving you is first on my list. Give me a grateful attitude so that I won't become preoccupied with wanting more."

by Lisa Cheater

The value of a Christian buddy ...

"Again I say to you, that if two of you agree on earth about anything that they may ask, it shall be done for them by My Father who is in Heaven." - **Matthew 18:19**

A true Christian friend can share happy times with you, but he or she can also serve as a fellow warrior in times of trouble. There is nothing more powerful than a friend who will pray with you and for you, no matter what the situation. When you ask someone to pray with you according to My will, I open the floodgates of Heaven's blessings!

Now what? *Pray:* "Jesus, why do I hold so many of my feelings and worries inside when you have provided Christian friends and leaders to pray with me? Your word promises that you will do whatever another Believer agrees with me needs fixing as long as it lines up with your teaching in scripture! Help me trade hopelessness for courage to ask someone to pray with me the next time I feel like I'm up against a wall."

347

Holy GPS . . .

"He guides the humble in what is right and teaches them his way. All the ways of the LORD are loving and faithful for those who keep the demands of his covenant." - **Psalm 25:9-10 (NIV)**

If you became lost in an unfamiliar town, you wouldn't hesitate to switch on your GPS or phone to get your bearings. You have faith that the maps in the system are correct and will get you safely home. Have that same kind of faith in Me when you become discouraged, confused, or challenged in life! My teachings and holy scripture will give you the answers you need to lead you out of any problem.

Now what? *Pray:* "Lord, I need direction. There are so many demands upon my time by friends, family, school, and even church that I often forget important commitments or are too tired to carry them out. Where do you want me to go? What do you want me to do? How should I spend my time? Lead me, Lord, along the path you've chosen for me. Give me clarity today to make the right decisions."

by Lisa Cheater

The loudest voice is the softest ...

"If anyone thinks himself to be religious, and yet does not bridle his tongue but deceives his own heart, this man's religion is worthless."
- **James 1:26**

Being a Christian doesn't give you permission to viciously attack, judge, or slander another person. You may feel entitled, you may even be right, but you cannot forget all the scriptures that guide your behavior. Nothing tells more about a person's heart than they words they speak. The world is desperate to find something different in you, something that proves I am real! Hold your tongue when you are tempted to blast out in a tirade. Your self-control will speak so much louder than your shouts.

Now what? *Pray:* Lord, I live in a culture where the loudest, strongest guy wins. It is so tempting to fall into that mindset when I'm being ridiculed, picked on or treated unfairly. Prevent me from launching into an argument every time I'm invited to one, just like some non-Believers would do. Strengthen my self-control so I can either offer a calm response or walk away."

349

Tough angels . . .

"For he will command his angels concerning you to guard you in all your ways." - **Psalms 91:11 (NIV)**

Angels are very real and they are among you every day. Unlike depictions on chapel walls, however, they are not small, squishy, childlike imps that flit about aimlessly. They are Heaven's warriors, mightily-armed ambassadors that have been given the task of protecting Christians. Countless times they have already steered you from potential harm. Offer thanks now for the guardians I have placed over you.

Now what? *Pray:* "Lord, thank you for the many angels that I have never seen moving around me, sheltering me and guiding me away from harm. That is so cool! I never have to feel like I'm battling evil or sin by myself. Whenever I cross into unfamiliar territory, let me remember that I am not alone. You and your army of winged warriors are all around me!"

by Lisa Cheater

It's all good …

"I have learned to be content in whatever circumstances I am." - **Philippians 4:11**

Can you say that? Or are you waiting for your situation to improve or change to the way you want it? Do you realize that Paul wrote these words while he was in prison for preaching about Me? Stop waiting for a different life! You are missing out on the blessings that I am sending you every single day! Yes, dream and seek My guidance about your future, but waste no more time longing for things to change. I am with you all the time and will take care of you. (BTW, Paul was set free by a guard who heard his preaching.)

Now what? *Pray:* "Lord, the hardest thing for me to realize is that life is not all about me, my comfort or my continual happiness. It's about serving you and leading others to know you. When I don't understand your plan or when it looks like I'm being unfairly accused, I will trust you and hold tight to your promises. Give me faith that you are looking out for me in all circumstances, to be content, and resist complaining."

351

Words to live by ...

"Your word is a lamp to my feet and a light to my path." - **Psalms 119:105**

What would it be like to find your way through an unfamiliar forest at night with no flashlight? Terrifying? Hopeless? Confusing? That's how it feels to live life without Me. The Bible serves to guide your walk through a difficult and dark world. Stop stumbling through your day hoping for a bit of good luck and things to make you happy. All you have to do is read The Word to understand how to navigate the many twisting paths of your life.

Now what? *Pray:* "Jesus, give me understanding of your Word to better apply what I read to my life. May it become just like a flashlight in the dark, illuminating the steps I should take and the right way to turn. Thank you for giving us the Bible as a guide for our lives. Increase my ability to understand and recall scripture so its promises stay with me at all times."

by Lisa Cheater

Solid future...

"Commit your works to the LORD, and your plans will be established."-
Proverbs 16:3

I have so many wonderful things in store for you! Each day is another opportunity for you to receive my blessings, but be careful about asking Me to approve plans you've already made without My assistance. Running headlong into something that you want to do guided by ambition or selfishness will result in disaster. Consult Me first in everything, and you will succeed according to My plans.

Now what? *Pray:* "Jesus, there are so many things I want to accomplish. One of my greatest dreams is to: ____(name it)____. Is this something you want me to do? Is it a goal that will bring you glory and help others or is it an aspiration motivated by selfishness or revenge? Fine-tune my ambitions so they align with your will and make the best use of my unique skills."

353

Turnaround King . . .

"As for you, you meant evil against me, but God meant it for good in order to bring about this present result, to preserve many people alive."-
Genesis 50:20

Satan is always looking for ways to make you stumble, but even when he succeeds, I have the power to bring good from evil. Only I know what the future holds for you and how the enemy's schemes can actually turn into a positive. Think how many countries gained independence after a war, how many people accepted Me because of a crisis in their life, and how many ministries have been started because of an illness or injury! There is hope in every situation.

Now what? *Pray:* Jesus, I am awed by your creative problem solving. Only you can bring beauty out of ashes. Help me to see the bigger picture of my life, and that some difficult situations I'm facing now will result in a tremendous victory later on. I will not become disheartened by difficult challenges because with you anything is possible."

by Lisa Cheater

Ban the tantrums...

"When I was a child, I talked like a child, I thought like a child, I reasoned like a child. When I became a man, I put childish ways behind me." - **1 Corinthians 13:11 (NIV)**

Do you have any recollection of being a three-year old? Most toddlers respond to problems by throwing a monumental fit, sometimes in public, much to the dismay of mom and dad. Small kids don't yet have the skills to reason, especially when they are angry. You are *not* a little kid anymore. You *do* have the ability to assess challenges and respond calmly. When you don't get your way, don't revert back to the Happy Meal days!

Now what? *Pray:* "Jesus, I admit that letting go of old habits can be a little scary. In fact, one childish behavior I still hang on to is ____(name it)____. I shouldn't be embarrassed; you know all about it already. Lord, take this behavior from me and replace it with the fruits of your spirit: love, joy, peace, kindness, goodness, faithfulness, patience, and self-control. The grown-up respect I long for is given to those with these qualities. You are the perfect example."

355

God's warehouse is full . . .

"Bless the LORD, O my soul, and all that is within me, bless His holy name." - **Psalms 103:1**

Imagine a huge pile of presents beneath your Christmas tree, all labeled to you! To open a gift, all you have to do is ask your parent for one. Would you just look at the gifts, wondering what's inside, then walk away and forget about them? No way! Likewise, I have a storehouse of blessings that I desire to give you, all waiting to be opened. To get delivery, all you have to do is ask Me!

Now what? *Pray:* "Oh, Lord, thank you for setting aside a very special set of blessings just for me! Yes, I want all you've got for me, all the best of an abundant life. You see my future clearly and already know exactly which gifts I should have. You always fill my needs, Lord. You're better than a personal shopper! Give me faith to trust you with how and when you choose to bless me."

by Lisa Cheater

356

Proof I am Lord...

"Therefore the Lord Himself will give you a sign: Behold, a virgin will be with child and bear a son, and she will call His name Immanuel." - **Isaiah 7:14**

You know this story. You know about the prophets who talked about how the Jewish Messiah would be born of a virgin and suffer under soldiers, die, and then be resurrected. I fulfilled every prophecy, details that were scribed thousands of years before My birth, but there are still many Jews who are waiting for their Messiah to come. I am already here! Pray today that your Jewish friends will come to accept Me as their Lord.

Now what? *Pray:* "Jesus, my heart breaks for my Jewish friends and acquaintances who have not accepted that you are their Messiah, too. I pray that each one of them will soften their hearts toward you and will seek out what it means to be a Jewish Christian; they *can* be both. Give me the words to say if necessary, and help me show them the respect they deserve as your chosen people. Let my attitude pique their interest in a relationship with you."

357

Joyous Day!

"For a child will be born to us, a son will be given to us; And the government will rest on His shoulders; And His name will be called Wonderful Counselor, Mighty God, Eternal Father, Prince of Peace."-**Isaiah 9:6**

When Christmas finally rolls around, and you are surrounded by presents, cookies and turkey, remember to think about the gifts I have sent you. Counsel – I guide you through the Bible and through other Believers. Mighty God – I am your Warrior in battle! Eternal Life – Unlike your iPod or phone, I never require charging. Peace – No drug can ever bring you peace like My presence. I am the Gift that keeps giving.

Now what? *Pray:* " Jesus, I'm so glad you were born! I don't want to wait for Christmas to give you the very best gift I have to offer: my life. I give to you my plans, my control, my behavior, my speech, my thoughts, my actions—everything is yours. You are worthy of my all because you gave your all for me. You give every person on the earth hope and a reason to love, and for that, I love you, Jesus."

by Lisa Cheater

358

Nothing hidden ...

"You know when I sit down and when I rise up; You understand my thought from afar." - **Psalms 139:2**

The bad news: I know everything you do. The good news: I know everything you do. Unlike your parents, I am always with you and see everything you say and think. I see inside the mask you put on to fool other people. But that's a good thing, too, because I already know all about the *real* you. I hear your cries for help, and I know your heart when you want to accomplish something. When you wish someone could just "get you," remember I've already "got you."

Now what? *Pray:* "Lord, I find myself constantly saying to my parents or certain friends, 'you just don't understand.' But you do. I don't have to pretend to be somebody else or to act a certain way around you. You see all my faults and yet you still love me. Jesus, if I had to cut to the very center of my heart right now, it would reveal this deep, nagging ache: _____(name it)_____. Lift this burden from me, Lord, and show me the best way to handle it."

Strength in weakness . . .

"My grace is sufficient for you, for power is perfected in weakness." -
2 Corinthians 12:9a

It's no fun to fall down, but sometimes, it's necessary. When you were very small and just learning to walk, your parents allowed you to stumble a few times. They knew that if they picked you up every time, you'd never develop the strength in your leg muscles to walk on your own. When you feel defeated, lean on Me, especially if I choose not to immediately remove a problem for you. It means you are growing.

Now what? *Pray:* "Jesus, help me see that a fail in my eyes may be a lesson in yours. Don't let me become discouraged when I stumble and make the wrong choices. When I feel weak and emotionally exhausted, lift me to my feet again, Lord. May I always turn to you as my source of strength, enragement and perseverance to keep going."

by Lisa Cheater

Prayer for a good day ...

"Let the words of my mouth and the meditation of my heart be acceptable in Your sight, O LORD, my rock and my Redeemer." - **Psalms 19:14**

The measure of a good day is not the absence of challenges, but rather your wise response to each problem. When this verse represents the desire of your heart, you will experience peace like none other because you are focused on pleasing Me rather than being free from stress. You may not have a perfect day, but with My help, you will maintain your self-control and avoid the anxiety that results from despair and critical thinking.

Now what? *Pray:* "Lord, no matter what today brings, may I hold to this scripture. I want you to find my words and thoughts pleasing, an outward demonstration of an inward commitment. Thank you, Lord."

Um . . . I don't get it . . .

"For now we see in a mirror dimly, but then face to face; now I know in part, but then I will know fully just as I also have been fully known." -
1 Corinthians 13:12

I can see all you do, all that's happening around you, but you can only see My outlines, murky glimpses of Me as you trust Me to guide you in the right way. I'm not trapped behind a glass, though, and I can intervene to help you. Someday, when you are with Me in Heaven, you will see Me and all My purposes for everything. And it will all make sense then. Trust means you don't need proof and all the answers right now to believe in Me.

> Now what? *Pray:* "Jesus, you are awesome and wonderful, loving and wise, yet so much about you is a mystery. I don't know why things happen the way they do, why there is suffering, or what impact I will have in the world. But I do know, in time, you will answer all my questions. Until then, keep me focused on living the Light that is within me."

by Lisa Cheater

Performance review . . .

"Let me hear Your loving-kindness in the morning; For I trust in You; Teach me the way in which I should walk; For to You I lift up my soul."-
Psalms 143:8

I am so proud of you for committing to spending time with Me in prayer and scripture. How're you doing? In what area of your life are you still struggling with sin? There's no need to criticize yourself, just be honest. Acknowledging your faults is the first step in fixing them! Think up a codeword for your most challenging sin so only you and I will know what it means. Write that word down in the back of your Bible or keep it on your dresser as a reminder to keep working on it. I believe in you.

Now what? *Pray:* "Jesus, despite my efforts I am still struggling with this sin: ____(name it)____. I know it's wrong and goes against your teaching, but it's as if this habit has been programmed into me. Please help me break this cycle of sin! The codeword I will give this problem is: ____(name any word—*come on, be creative*)____. I will write this code someplace where I will see it every morning and remember that you are by my side, helping me overcome my temptations."

363

Step out of your comfort zone . . .

"Do not say, 'I am only a child.' You must go to everyone I send you to and say whatever I command you. Do not be afraid of them, for I am with you and will rescue you!" - **Jeremiah 1:7-8 (NIV)**

Your comfort zone is made up of things you see and do all the time, places you always go and people you always talk to. You rarely feel afraid inside your comfort zone, but sometimes I need you to venture out beyond the safety of those walls. Maybe you feel Me asking you to talk to a new student at school, invite a friend to church, go on a mission trip, or fess up to a destructive behavior. You might feel nervous about it at first, but remember I am always with you! Each time you step out to obey Me, your faith grows stronger.

Now What? *Pray:* "Jesus, thank you for constantly presenting me with new ways to grow and mature. I often feel like I'm lost somewhere between being an adult and feeling like a little kid, and I need your clear direction and courage to help me step out of my comfort zone. Calm my nervous fears, and teach me to obey your requests with joy."

by Lisa Cheater

364

Touchdown!

"My inmost being will rejoice when your lips speak what is right." - **Proverbs 23:16**

What is your favorite sport to watch on television? You probably don't know the individual players you're cheering on, but you anxiously study their every move, hoping they'll make the right play, catch, or move. When they score, you can't help but shout! That's exactly how I feel when you are in a situation that calls for you to take a stand for Me. When you say something kind or encouraging to someone, gently correct a pal according to My scripture, or defend the downtrodden, I cheer out loud! I'm watching you, dear child, and here to help you do your best.

Now what? *Pray?* Jesus, sometimes I feel like only my mistakes get noticed, but I'm so glad to know you see the good things I do. Encourage me to keep following your Word even if I don't get a pat on the back or acknowledgement from others. You see me. You know. You'll reward me with blessing. And that's all that matters."

Mine to love ...

"Now may our Lord Jesus Christ Himself and God our Father, who has loved us and given us eternal comfort and good hope by grace, comfort and strengthen your hearts in every good work and word." -
1 Thessalonians 2:16-17

Never forget how much I love you, how important you are to Me, and that I have a special purpose for your life. What's the next step in your Christian walk? Repairing a difficult relationship? Memorizing scripture? Committing to daily quiet time or a mission trip? Make that your goal for the next phase of your discipleship!

Now what? *Pray:* "Jesus, just like sports or academics, growing as a Christian takes diligence, practice and vision for where I should be. Give me clarity and honesty as I plan spiritual goals for this next year. Tell me where you want me to focus my skills, volunteer time, and learning, and protect me from the enemy who may try to keep me from moving forward. Wherever you lead, Jesus, I am willing to go."

Made in the USA
Middletown, DE
01 May 2023